WALK WITH JESUS

BIBLE STUDY FOR WOMEN

ALSO BY HELEN H. LEE, MSc

Finding Peace: Prayer Journal for Women:
Weekly Devotions, Prompts, and Exercises for Managing Anxiety

WALK
WITH
JESUS

BIBLE STUDY FOR WOMEN

A Year of Teachings and Prayers to Grow in Faith and Love

HELEN H. LEE, MSc

ZEITGEIST · NEW YORK

TO JESUS CHRIST, WHO, THROUGH THE
GREATEST ACT OF LOVE, SAVED ME
BY PAYING THE PENALTY FOR ALL MY
SINS—PAST, PRESENT, AND FUTURE

Published in the United States by Zeitgeist, an imprint of Zeitgeist™,
a division of Penguin Random House LLC, New York.
zeitgeistpublishing.com

ISBN: 9780593690222

Book design by Emma Hall
Author photograph © by Grace Lee
Edited by Caroline Lee

Printed in the United States of America
2nd Printing

INTRODUCTION

You may have started flipping through these pages because you're searching for new ways to infuse your daily life with God's Word. Or maybe you are yearning for spiritual nourishment and determined to deepen your faith. Perhaps you're facing a challenging situation and the load feels heavy to carry on your own, so you're longing for a greater sense of God's presence. Maybe you're desiring to step into God's purpose for you—or feeling weary and looking to find rest for your soul. Regardless of what season you may find yourself in, this devotional was written for the woman seeking spiritual growth and a clearer sense of God's will for her life.

My deepest desire for you is that you discover Jesus' true nature in these pages and experience his close presence and infinite love for you, whether you are just beginning your journey in faith or can confidently declare yourself a mature believer. As you connect with Jesus, I pray his devotion for you stirs your heart and deepens your desire to know him. God has a purpose for your life, and you are valuable in his sight. He created you with unique gifts and calls you to use them for his glory.

This Bible study is your invitation to reflect on and learn about Jesus' qualities so you can imitate him in your own walk with God. By exploring Jesus' life, teachings, identity, death, resurrection, and impact on our lives, this Bible study aims to equip you with a solid foundation for living out your faith. I hope it will plant seeds and propel deep spiritual growth so you can bloom and flourish as the woman God has called you to be.

HOW TO USE THIS BOOK

It can be challenging to unpack all of the rich meaning from Scripture's many layers. Let's explore some ways to study the Bible, develop a deeper relationship with God, and weave what you learn into your everyday life.

ENCOUNTERING JESUS IN YOUR BIBLE STUDY

The Bible is a sacred and living text inspired by God. Even though it was written long ago, it is timeless, filled with lessons relevant for today that can transform our hearts and lives. The Word is essential to our spiritual growth and nourishment (Matthew 4:4; 1 Peter 2:2). Looking to Scripture prepares us to face struggles with faith and confidence (Ephesians 6:17), guides our path (Psalm 119:105), and equips us to live out God's plan for us.

Here are some helpful tips for studying the Bible:

BEGIN WITH PRAYER—Ask God to guide your understanding of his Word. Be open, curious, and willing to allow the Holy Spirit to guide you.

BE CONSISTENT—Study the Bible with others, but be sure to dedicate some quiet time for yourself to be in the Word daily. Consider starting with a few minutes and gradually increase the time you spend studying. Sneak in some reading whenever you have a free moment. If you miss some days, just jump back in wherever you left off.

INCORPORATE STRUCTURE—Find a way to study the Bible that helps you maintain a sense of order and structure. For example, read one specific book of the Bible at a time, follow a study like this one, or read a supplementary commentary for a guided study.

OBSERVE, REFLECT, AND APPLY—After reading a passage, take some time to reflect on it. Then think of ways to apply what you've read to your life.

AVOID TAKING VERSES OUT OF CONTEXT—Rather than isolating a single verse and overgeneralizing the concept behind it, take time to understand the biblical context of a passage to interpret it most accurately. Something that can help with this is to cross-reference other verses in the Bible related to the verses you are reading.

THE BASICS

This study focuses on the first four books of the New Testament—Matthew, Mark, Luke, and John—collectively called the Gospels. *Gospel* refers to the good news that Jesus died on the cross to pay the penalty for our sins so we can have eternal life through faith in him. This is a gift, given to us through grace rather than earned by our own effort or merit (Ephesians 2:8–9). By rising from the dead, Jesus demonstrated his power over sin and death (1 Corinthians 15:17), once and for all.

The Gospels provide historical accounts of the life, teachings, death, and resurrection of Jesus. Each provides a different perspective: **Matthew** emphasizes Jesus' genealogy and the fulfillment through Jesus of what the Old Testament foretold so that the Jewish population of the time could recognize him as the promised Messiah. **Mark** was written for Gentiles, or non-Jewish believers, and focuses on Jesus' actions and miracles as a servant of God. **Luke** describes Jesus as the Son of man and illustrates his character through stories of his compassion for the needy, the sick, and the outcast. **John** emphasizes Jesus' divine nature as the Son of God and his role in our salvation. When combined, these four sacred texts give us a rich and harmonious depiction of Jesus' life and ministry.

KEY FEATURES

WEEKLY THEME

This 52-week Bible study is designed to help you deepen your faith and grow closer to Jesus. By consistently getting into the Word, you will come to see how Jesus' teachings apply to our everyday lives in the modern world. An overarching weekly theme is broken down into daily readings, giving you an opportunity to spend a little time each day studying and applying Scripture to different areas of your life.

READINGS AND BIBLE STUDY

Set aside time daily to follow the reading plan. You'll read a short passage on six days of the week, then use day 7 to delve into the Bible study and the prompts—either on your own or with a group. Each lesson includes tips for incorporating the weekly theme into your life and actively applying what you've learned.

PROMPTS

Use the prompts to draw deeper meaning from Jesus' words and actions.

- "Observe" prompts provided in this yearlong Bible study are meant to set the scene and provide contextual understanding of the Scripture.

- "Reflect" prompts encourage you to look inward and discern how God might be speaking into your life through Scripture.

- "Apply" prompts are meant to help you identify and live out what God is calling you to do in practical and actionable ways.

   Use the writing space and margins for your personal reflections and prayers. To get the best results from this Bible study, find a quiet and comfortable place to write, set aside dedicated time to complete each reading, and pray for guidance and understanding before beginning.

DAILY PRAYERS

Prayer is a gift and privilege to help us connect with God. Take every opportunity to communicate with him, and he will guide you throughout your day. Use the provided prayers as encouragement to develop your own personal prayer life with God.

RECAP AND KEY VERSES

The recaps and Scripture verses are designed to keep the week's main takeaways in the front of your mind, even when life gets busy. Remember that even small moments of reading, reflection, and prayer can make a significant difference in your daily life.

The Good News: God's Divine Intentions

Reading Plan

DAY 1: Luke 1:1–38

DAY 2: John 1:1–14

DAY 3: Matthew 1:1–25

DAY 4: Luke 3:23–38

DAY 5: Luke 1:39–66

DAY 6: Luke 1:67–80

DAY 7: Study and Reflection

Bible Study

In the books of Matthew and Luke, we see that what the Old Testament fore-shadowed about Jesus came true—he descended from the lineage of Abraham and King David. John 1 explains that Jesus was with God from the beginning and has always been one with God. The beauty of these passages, when taken together, is that they demonstrate the fact that Jesus was both human and divine at once and that God orchestrated his divine plan long before Jesus' birth. In his humanity, Jesus experienced temptation, suffering, and death. In his divinity, as God's own Son free from sin, Jesus was able to serve as the mediator between God and humanity.

The story leading up to Jesus' birth may be so familiar that it would be easy to overlook how intentional God was to fulfill his plan, down to the last detail. There have been many times in my life when I looked back and saw God's perfect wisdom and intentionality in how events unfolded in my relationships, my work life, and ministry. When we can appreciate all the intricate details that needed to happen for God to fulfill his plan of salvation, we can take comfort in knowing that God also devised a divine plan for our lives with the same level of detail.

Prayer

Dear heavenly Father, thank you for sending your Son Jesus, to take the penalty for my sins. Guide me in the way of your perfect will in my life. In Jesus' name I pray. Amen.

Prompts, Reflections, Actions

OBSERVE

- What did the genealogies in Matthew 1 and Luke 3 show about Jesus' lineage?

- What is the significance of Jesus as both fully God and fully human?

- In Luke 1, Mary receives news that she will give birth to Jesus. What is her response?

REFLECT

- So many intricate details were fulfilled for Jesus' birth to take place. What does that reveal to you about God's nature and his desire to save you?

- When you are reminded of God's divine plan for your salvation, how does that help you to trust God's intentionality in all aspects of your personal life?

APPLY

- Describe your response to knowing that God sent his one and only Son to save you.

- What role does Jesus play in your life as your personal Savior?

Week Recap

The passages from this week reveal the divine plan God orchestrated long before Jesus' birth, demonstrating his intentionality and faithfulness to his promises. We are reminded of God's incredible love for us and the lengths he went to so that we could be saved.

For with God nothing shall be impossible.

LUKE 1:37 (KJV)

TRUST IN GOD'S PROVIDENCE AND PROTECTION

Reading Plan

DAY 1: Luke 2:1–7

DAY 2: Luke 2:8–20

DAY 3: Luke 2:21–39

DAY 4: Matthew 2:1–12

DAY 5: Matthew 2:13–18

DAY 6: Matthew 2:19–23

DAY 7: Study and Reflection

Bible Study

When we lose sight of God's goodness and faithfulness, it's easy to fall into fear and act out of self-preservation rather than look for God's presence and guidance. Maybe you've been in a situation where it's easy to focus on how impossible your circumstances appear. During these times, we may respond by trying to take control, looking for a quick solution, or making decisions on what makes sense from our point of view rather than seeking God's guidance and remembering that he's watching out for us.

As you look back over this week's readings, you'll see how God demonstrated his providence and protection over Jesus despite the dangers surrounding his birth. Before Jesus was born, his parents, Joseph and Mary, were required to journey from Nazareth to Bethlehem, as Caesar Augustus, the ruler of the Roman world, was taking a census. As a descendant of King David, Joseph had to take his young, pregnant wife, go to Bethlehem—the city of David—and be registered there. When Jesus was born, this fulfilled the Old Testament prophecy that the Messiah—the long-awaited Savior—would come from the line of David and be born in Bethlehem.

Meanwhile, from far in the East, the wise men also journeyed to Bethlehem, searching for the expected Savior. When King Herod heard about this, he felt threatened and tried to stop Jesus' birth, eventually resorting to the murder of baby boys in Bethlehem who were two years or younger. But after Jesus' birth, God's angel instructed Joseph to take Mary and the baby and flee to safety in Egypt until they could return home to Nazareth after Herod's death.

Can you imagine a more dangerous beginning than Jesus'? Just like God protected Jesus, he is also our protector. Let this story remind you that nothing can thwart God's perfect plans, and rest easy knowing that he is with you, ready to defend, protect, and guide you.

Prayer

Dear heavenly Father, thank you for your providence and protection in my life. Help me to remember that nothing can hinder your plans and that you're always watching over me. In Jesus' name I pray. Amen.

Prompts, Reflections, Actions

OBSERVE

- What event ensured that Jesus would be born in Bethlehem?

- In Matthew 2, how did Herod attempt to stop God's plans?

- How did God use angels in the events that took place in Luke 2 and Matthew 2?

REFLECT

- When did you last experience fear? How did you react? Did you rely on God's presence and seek his guidance or take matters into your own hands?

- Where in your own life have you recently experienced God's faithfulness? How can that memory fuel you going forward?

- How can reflecting on God's providence and protection over Jesus' birth help you trust in God's plan for your own life?

APPLY

- What would it look like if you were to rely more on God's protection and providence in your life? List some practical steps you can take to nurture that sense of reliance.

- What can you to do avoid giving in to fear when you are facing challenges in your life?

Week Recap

We see God's providence and protection over Jesus in the events surrounding his birth. Despite many threats, God guided Joseph and Mary to Bethlehem and protected Jesus from King Herod's plan to kill him. We can find comfort in God's faithfulness, trusting that we are never alone and that God will defend and protect us as his children.

And the angel said unto them, Fear not: for, behold,
I bring you good tidings of great joy, which shall be
to all people. For unto you is born this day in the city
of David a Saviour, which is Christ the Lord.

LUKE 2:10–11 (KJV)

PREPARING THE WAY:
REPENTANCE LEADS TO FREEDOM

Reading Plan

DAY 1: Luke 2:40–47

DAY 2: Luke 2:48–52

DAY 3: Matthew 3:1–12

DAY 4: Mark 1:1–8

DAY 5: Luke 3:1–18

DAY 6: John 1:15–28

DAY 7: Study and Reflection

Bible Study

In this week's readings, we see John the Baptist preparing the way for the coming of Jesus' earthly ministry. John shares the importance of repentance with the people of Israel. Repentance involves feeling sorrow for offending God with our sin. Sin is anything that goes against God's law or any kind of rebellion against God. As we learn in this week's readings, repenting and accepting Jesus into our lives as our Savior allows us to be forgiven and freed.

Repentance isn't always easy, though. Truly repenting involves expressing our sorrow to God for going against him. Repentance is when we desire to move away from our sin and toward God and what he desires for us. The sorrow that comes with repentance is different from feeling embarrassed we got caught or being afraid of getting punished. When we refuse to acknowledge our sin to God, we cannot receive God's mercy and forgiveness.

Fortunately, the Holy Spirit is always there to help us be aware of our need to repent and walk according to God's will. There are times when I've used a harsh tone with my family members or held unforgiveness in my heart. I've resisted repenting because I didn't want to admit that I was in the wrong. But God gently reminds us that he doesn't expect us to be perfect. He asks that we approach him with a humble and repentant heart so we can receive his forgiveness immediately and experience deep intimacy with him. This allows the Holy Spirit to transform our hearts from the inside and experience freedom from our sins. When we remember this, repentance is no longer something to avoid because it results in forgiveness and freedom.

Prayer

Dear heavenly Father, please reveal to me my sins, any wrong ways of thinking, and errors in my ways that go against you. Please forgive me and transform my heart so that I can walk in your ways and in your will. Help me see that I need you as my Savior. In Jesus' name I pray. Amen.

Prompts, Reflections, Actions

OBSERVE

- What message did John the Baptist preach to the Jewish people?

- In Luke 3, what practical advice did John give to people who came to repent and receive forgiveness? Is that still sound advice today?

- In Mark 1:7, John says that someone more powerful than himself is coming soon. Who is John referring to?

REFLECT

- How does repentance prepare your heart to receive Jesus' forgiveness?

- Have you experienced freedom and forgiveness from confessing your sins? Describe your experience.

- Think about anything that might be weighing on your heart. How might asking for God's forgiveness lighten your load?

- How does being prideful keep us from seeking forgiveness, and how can we hold ourselves accountable?

Week Recap

John the Baptist prepared the way for Jesus' ministry by preaching a message of repentance. True repentance involves expressing our sorrow to God for going against him and intending to turn away from our sin—and when we do this, we can wholly receive God's forgiveness. The Holy Spirit can then work in our hearts and lives to transform us.

In those days came John the Baptist, preaching in the wilderness of Judaea, And saying, Repent ye: for the kingdom of heaven is at hand.

MATTHEW 3:1-2 (KJV)

God the Father, Son, and Holy Spirit

Reading Plan

DAY 1: Matthew 3:13–17

DAY 2: Mark 1:9–11

DAY 3: Luke 3:19–22

DAY 4: John 1:32–34

DAY 5: John 1:35–42

DAY 6: John 1:43–51

DAY 7: Study and Reflection

Bible Study

At Jesus' baptism, the Holy Trinity—God the Father, God the Son, and God the Holy Spirit—was revealed. As Jesus rose from the water, the Father's voice proclaimed that this was his Son, and the Spirit, in the form of a dove, descended from above.

Because each person of the Trinity is fully God and equally God, connecting with the Father, the Son, and the Holy Spirit draws us into a more complete and fulfilling relationship with God.

God the Father—our creator, provider, protector, and the one we pray to—comforts and disciplines us as a loving Father. When we see God as a

Father, we can relate to him as his beloved children. We can go to him for everything we need, knowing that it pleases him to care for us.

There is Jesus, God's Son, our Savior—and it is through and because of him that we can have direct access and a restored relationship with God the Father. He is at the right hand of the Father, advocating for us every day.

And there is the Holy Spirit, who resides within each of us when we are born again. The Holy Spirit informs our spiritual knowledge, transforms us to walk according to God's will, and guides us. We can rely on the Holy Spirit to comfort us until Jesus' return, when we are physically united with God.

Connect with each person of the Trinity, as it can be easy to focus on one and overlook another. For example, those of us who may have felt emotionally neglected or abandoned by our earthly father may find it difficult to connect with God as our heavenly Father. Fortunately, God's love as a Father is perfect even when our earthly father is unable to meet our need for love. By getting to know each person of the Trinity, we can experience the fullness of God's love, grace, and power in our lives.

Prayer

Dear heavenly Father, thank you for the gift of baptism
and the Holy Trinity. Help me to connect with you, Father,
Son, and Holy Spirit, so that I can know you better and
grow deeper in my faith. In Jesus' name I pray. Amen.

Prompts, Reflections, Actions

OBSERVE

- At Jesus' baptism, what did God say?

- Who baptized Jesus?

- What does Jesus' baptism reveal about God's nature?

REFLECT

- How has your understanding of the Trinity impacted your relationship with God? Is there one person of the Trinity that you find it harder or easier to connect to?

- How can you learn to rely more on the Holy Spirit to guide and empower you in your daily life?

APPLY

- Baptism symbolizes the washing away of our sins and the beginning of a new life in Christ. It also signifies Christ's death and resurrection as we are buried with him in the water and raised to new life in him. Baptism publicly lets others know of our new identity in Christ—an outward expression of an inward change. If you have been baptized, what did it mean to you?

- If you have not yet been baptized, what steps can you take toward deciding about being baptized?

- Think of some new ways to deepen your personal relationship with God, the Holy Spirit, and Jesus. How might they affect your daily life?

Week Recap

At Jesus' baptism, God's nature as one being but three distinct persons was demonstrated: God the Father; Jesus, the Son of God; and the Holy Spirit. We may find it hard to connect with all three persons of the Trinity equally, but developing a relationship with each—God the Father, the Son, and the Holy Spirit—can lead us into a richer, more fulfilling relationship with God.

And Jesus, when he was baptized, went up straightway
out of the water: and, lo, the heavens were opened unto
him, and he saw the Spirit of God descending like a dove,
and lighting upon him: And lo a voice from heaven, saying,
This is my beloved Son, in whom I am well pleased.

MATTHEW 3:16–17 (KJV)

TRIAL IN THE WILDERNESS: CONQUERING TEMPTATION

Reading Plan

DAY 1: Matthew 4:1–4

DAY 2: Matthew 4:5–11

DAY 3: Mark 1:12–13

DAY 4: Luke 4:1–8

DAY 5: Luke 4:9–13

DAY 6: John 2:1–11

DAY 7: Study and Reflection

Bible Study

Temptation is a part of life. Whether we're tempted to lust, give in to our pride or greed, compare ourselves with others, or gossip, we encounter temptation often—but we have a choice to submit to it or receive God's help to endure it.

It's all too easy to justify giving in to our temptation to relieve ourselves of the pain we may be suffering. When certain temptations arise over and over again, there may be something that God is asking us to address. He may be asking us to bring a past wound to him for healing or to remove ourselves from an environment that isn't fertile to our spiritual growth. Being tempted is not a sin, but it can be a signal to pay attention to an area that God may want us to mature in.

Even Jesus faced temptation, and in this week's readings, we learn about how he responded to it. Jesus could easily have defeated Satan using his divine powers in the wilderness but instead chose to use Scripture to overcome each temptation. Good news: we all have access to those same Scriptures.

Isn't that amazing? God provides us with the same Scriptures that Jesus used to overcome temptation so we can find true freedom. We can meditate on the truth found in God's Word to renew our minds. Through this renewal, our thoughts, desires, and actions become more aligned to God's will so we can live in spiritual victory.

Prayer

Dear heavenly Father, help me recognize areas in my life where I'm vulnerable to temptation. Renew my mind with your truth and give me victory over sin. In Jesus' name I pray. Amen.

Prompts, Reflections, Actions

OBSERVE

- While Jesus was fasting in the wilderness, what did Satan do?

- How did Jesus respond to each of Satan's temptations?

- How did Satan react to Jesus' responses?

REFLECT

- What kinds of temptation do you struggle with the most? How can being aware of that lead you to experience freedom?

APPLY

- Navigate your temptation: What are the circumstances, actions, routines, and attitudes that tend to activate temptation in your life? Ask God to help you devise strategies to deal with the next time you're tempted, and write the strategies down. Share with a confidant, recruit help, or seek support from a trusted source (e.g., friend or leader at church).

- Renew your mind with Scriptures and find verses that speak to areas where you experience temptation. Meditate on these verses, pray, and worship daily to focus your thoughts on God.

Week Recap

Jesus responded to Satan's temptation with Scripture. Similarly, we can renew our minds by meditating on God's Word and using it to help us resist temptation to move forward in spiritual victory.

And when the tempter came to him, he said, If thou be the Son of God, command that these stones be made bread. But he answered and said, It is written, Man shall not live by bread alone, but by every word that proceedeth out of the mouth of God.

MATTHEW 4:3-4 (KJV)

WEEK 6

BEING REBORN: A CALL TO NEW LIFE

Reading Plan

DAY 1: John 2:12–18

DAY 2: John 2:18–25

DAY 3: John 3:1–11

DAY 4: John 3:12–21

DAY 5: John 3:22–29

DAY 6: John 3:30–36

DAY 7: Study and Reflection

Bible Study

It was late at night when Nicodemus, an official from the Jewish ruling council, crept through the darkness to visit Jesus. He'd heard about Jesus' teachings and wanted to know more—but he didn't want to be seen by the other Pharisees. Jesus told Nicodemus that to enter God's kingdom, one must be born again by believing in God's one and only begotten Son. Nicodemus was bewildered about the idea of being reborn and wondered how such a thing could be possible.

Being born again means we are a new creation in Christ, marking the beginning of a whole transformation of mind and heart. However, this does not mean we will never see parts of our old self creep back in at times. Even though our old tendencies may make an appearance from time to time, being reborn means that we are no longer condemned for our sin and no longer defined by our past or how the world sees us. In our past, we may have seen ourselves as broken, unloved, and unworthy, but in Christ, we are free, loved, and whole. In this newness of life, God equips us with spiritual knowledge, understanding, and the gifts we'll need to fully live out our new identity and life in Christ. Being reborn means gaining a new awareness, new habits, and a new outlook—and those things bring us purpose and freedom. Living as a born-again daughter of God is a lifelong journey that will require continual and intentional steps to seek him, allow him to shape our identity, and live out his love daily.

Prayer

Dear heavenly Father, thank you for showing me the path to rebirth and new life. Give me spiritual understanding and walk with me in my renewed life. In Jesus' name I pray. Amen.

Prompts, Reflections, Actions

OBSERVE

- Why did Nicodemus come to Jesus in John 3?

- What did Jesus say to Nicodemus about being born again in John 3?

- What does it mean to be born again according to Jesus in John 3?

- It's natural to struggle with aspects of faith. Grappling with your beliefs is an important part of your faith journey—it can meaningfully serve to draw you closer to God. What aspects of your faith are you currently struggling with?

- How has Christ transformed your life?

APPLY

- If you have experienced a renewed life in Christ, have you ever shared your testimony with others? If so, how did you begin? If not, how would you begin your story?

Week Recap

When Nicodemus seeks to learn from Jesus, he is told that he must be born again to see the kingdom of God. Jesus explains that being reborn means believing in him as God's one and only Son, who gives us everlasting life. We are transformed into Christ's image through the power of the Holy Spirit.

Jesus answered and said unto him, Verily, verily, I say unto thee, Except a man be born again, he cannot see the kingdom of God. Nicodemus saith unto him, How can a man be born when he is old? can he enter the second time into his mother's womb, and be born?

JOHN 3:3-4 (KJV)

LIVING WATER: NEVER THIRST AGAIN

Reading Plan

DAY 1: John 4:1–9

DAY 2: John 4:10–15

DAY 3: John 4:16–26

DAY 4: John 4:27–30

DAY 5: John 4:31–42

DAY 6: John 4:43–54

DAY 7: Study and Reflection

Bible Study

In John 4, Jesus is sitting on a well when he encounters a Samaritan woman who approaches to draw some water. She is surprised when he speaks to her, asking her for a drink. In those days, Jews did not typically interact with Samaritans. Jesus says that if she truly recognized him, she would ask *him* to serve her a drink, and he would offer her a different kind of water—living water. If she drank from it, she would never be thirsty again. After recognizing who Jesus is, the woman spreads the word about the Messiah, leading her entire village to believe.

Like the Samaritan woman who attempted to satisfy her heart through relationships, we often search in the wrong places to quench our soul's thirst. Many women I've worked with have tried to find their worth by pleasing others, only to feel deeply empty and unsatisfied inside. But once they find their worth in Christ, they find wholeness in him and no longer need to search for satisfaction in the wrong places. Just like the woman at the well, when we no longer focus on fulfilling ourselves, we can love from a pure heart and share Jesus' love with others.

Nothing this world offers can satisfy our deepest need—but the good news is that God can. The next time you feel that restless longing to quench your strongest thirst, remember that you are truly known and loved by the God who made you. Drink from the living water by spending time in God's Word, praying about your longings, and vulnerably sharing with him your struggles. Jesus can meet us in our brokenness and fulfill our profoundest desires. When we know that everything we could ever want or need is found in seeking and knowing God, we can be assured that we never have to thirst, ever again.

Prayer

Dear heavenly Father, please help me seek you above all else, knowing that you alone can quench my soul's thirst and satisfy my deepest longings. In Jesus' name I pray. Amen.

Prompts, Reflections, Actions

OBSERVE

- Why was the Samaritan woman surprised when Jesus asked her for a drink of water?

- What did the Samaritan woman do after realizing that Jesus was the Messiah?

- What secret did Jesus know about the Samaritan woman?

REFLECT

- Are there any relationships in your life that you rely on to feel fulfilled more than your relationship with God?

- In what ways can God satisfy your soul's thirst?

APPLY

- How can we shift focus toward seeking God and allowing him to fulfill us? Think of some practical steps you can take to seek and know God more deeply.

- The Samaritan woman invited others to experience Jesus for themselves. How can you share with others how God has quenched your thirst?

Week Recap

In John 4, Jesus offers living water to a Samaritan woman, revealing himself as the Messiah. Like the woman, we often search in the wrong places for fulfillment, but only God can quench our deepest thirst. God understands our longings, and his grace can bring eternal satisfaction and peace.

Jesus answered and said unto her, Whosoever drinketh
of this water shall thirst again: But whosoever drinketh
of the water that I shall give him shall never thirst;
but the water that I shall give him shall be in him a
well of water springing up into everlasting life.

JOHN 4:13–14 (KJV)

WEEK 8

A HUMBLE CALLING

Reading Plan

DAY 1: Matthew 4:12–17

DAY 2: Matthew 4:18–22

DAY 3: Mark 1:14–20

DAY 4: Luke 4:14–21

DAY 5: Luke 4:22–30

DAY 6: Luke 5:1–11

DAY 7: Study and Reflection

Bible Study

In Luke 5, Jesus uses Simon Peter's boat to preach to the gathered crowd on the beach. After preaching, he tells Simon to paddle out into deeper water and let down his nets. Simon points out that he and his fellow fishermen fished all night without a single catch, but he still obeys. What follows is a haul so big the boat begins to sink! Peter responds by falling to his knees before Jesus and proclaiming his own sinfulness. His humble response may have been a result of realizing his lack of faith and how good Jesus was.

This passage illustrates how God doesn't always show up in the ways we expect. Again and again, he chooses ordinary, flawed people like you and me to be his disciples. Jesus did not call on the powerful or elite but fishermen who were willing to follow him with humility and obedience.

We don't have to be perfect to be called by God. We only have to be humble, open, and willing. In our own lives, we can get swept up by the world's ways of seeking recognition, superiority over others, and self-promotion. But if we lack humility, we are likely to serve ourselves rather than depend on him. God knows humble people will give him the most glory and obey him rather than take the glory for themselves and insist on their own way.

Prayer

Dear heavenly Father, help me to follow you with a humble
and obedient heart, trusting that you can use me, just as I am,
to accomplish your will. In Jesus' name I pray. Amen.

Prompts, Reflections, Actions

OBSERVE

- What was Simon Peter's profession?

- What did Simon Peter call himself after the miraculous catch of fish?

- What did Jesus tell Simon they'd be doing going forward in Luke 5:10–11?

REFLECT

- Why is humility an important trait for those who desire to serve God?

- Has there been a time in your life when God used something or someone you considered insignificant to accomplish something great or unexpected? How did that experience impact your understanding of God's ability?

- Reflect on a time when you were hesitant to obey God's call but eventually chose to follow him. What influenced your decision? What was the result of your obedience?

APPLY

- What are some ways you can cultivate humility in your life, especially when it comes to serving others?

- Think of some ways you can use your talents and abilities to serve others, even if it means acting on seemingly small or insignificant tasks.

Week Recap

In Luke 5, Jesus uses Simon Peter's boat to preach to a crowd and commands him to let down his fishing nets, resulting in a miraculous catch. This passage demonstrates that God calls humble and obedient people to be his disciples.

And he saith unto them, Follow me, and I will make you fishers of men. And they straightway left their nets, and followed him.

MATTHEW 4:19–20 (KJV)

Jesus' Healing Touch

Reading Plan

DAY 1: Luke 4:31–44

DAY 2: Matthew 4:23–25

DAY 3: Mark 1:21–39

DAY 4: Luke 5:12–16

DAY 5: Matthew 8:1–4; Mark 1:40–45

DAY 6: Matthew 8:14–17

DAY 7: Study and Reflection

Bible Study

This week's readings reveal Jesus as an empathetic healer, unafraid to reach out and touch those who need him—even those rejected by society. A leper, for example, takes a risk in approaching Jesus, saying that he knows Jesus can heal him if he's willing. Even though leprosy is highly contagious and those with leprosy are considered outcasts, Jesus touches the leper, immediately healing him.

We, too, can acknowledge our need for healing and restoration in different areas of our lives, and we can trust that Jesus is always willing to meet us where we are and help us. Sometimes we may be reluctant to be vulnerable enough to ask for the help we need. Perhaps we feel unworthy or embarrassed.

But we can trust that we are not alone, even in our darkest moments. Jesus is right there beside us, and his presence in our lives can bring us healing and restoration. We may think that we need to clean ourselves up and be put together before we go to him. If there's an area of your life you haven't yet brought to him, remember that there's nothing that is beyond his grace to heal, forgive, and redeem.

Prayer

Dear heavenly Father, thank you for your willingness to heal and restore me. Help me to trust in your power and approach you with faith and humility. In Jesus' name I pray. Amen.

Prompts, Reflections, Actions

OBSERVE

- What did the leper say to Jesus before being healed?

- What did Jesus do after he withdrew into the wilderness in Luke 5:11?

- In Matthew 8:14–17, what did Jesus fulfill when he healed the sick and cast out demons?

REFLECT

- In what areas of your life do you need healing and restoration? Take time to acknowledge your need for Jesus and ask him to heal those areas.

- Reflect on any reluctance you may have to approach Jesus for help. What fears or beliefs may be holding you back?

APPLY

- Ask God to reveal the obstacles that keep you from going to him for help. What are some ways you can offer the most vulnerable version of yourself to Jesus?

- How can you demonstrate compassion and be a source of healing and support to people in your life and your community?

Week Recap

Jesus uses his divine power to heal many, including a leper who showed faith by approaching him despite being a social outcast. We, too, can approach Jesus—even in our brokenness—and trust in his healing and restoration.

And it came to pass, when he was in a certain city,
behold a man full of leprosy: who seeing Jesus fell
on his face, and besought him, saying, Lord, if thou
wilt, thou canst make me clean. And he put forth his
hand, and touched him, saying, I will: be thou clean.
And immediately the leprosy departed from him.

LUKE 5:12–13 (KJV)

Embracing New Wine with a New Heart

Reading Plan

DAY 1: Matthew 9:1–8

DAY 2: Matthew 9:9–17

DAY 3: Mark 2:1–12

DAY 4: Mark 2:13–22

DAY 5: Luke 5:17–26

DAY 6: Luke 5:27–39

DAY 7: Study and Reflection

Bible Study

Jesus demonstrated God's radical love for all people by ushering in a new way of thinking and living. The new way, or new wine, that Jesus introduced was the Gospel, which could not be mixed with the religious traditions of the time.

Before Jesus came into our lives, we may have had a way of thinking and doing things that kept us stuck in certain unhealthy cycles. There may be cultural or generational customs and beliefs that we used to follow that do not align with God's Word. I grew up in a culture where education and career, material wealth, and physical attractiveness were considered of utmost importance and celebrated. Even after finding Jesus, there were times I fell into patterns of prioritizing these things more than God.

In our old life, we may have been centered on ourselves and our own desires and ambitions without considering others' needs. Or we may have prioritized seeking our fulfillment through accumulating possessions. Or we may have believed lies about ourselves or fallen into thought patterns of fear, doubt, and self-condemnation. Replacing these patterns with God's ways doesn't happen overnight; parts of us want to cling to our old ways.

But if we want to experience the freedom Jesus' way of life offers and fully embrace the Gospel message, we must be willing to let go of our old ways and see the world and the people around us through our Father's eyes. Opening our minds to a new way can be difficult, but God can help us renew our minds when we are open to immersing ourselves in the truth found in his Word.

Prayer

Dear heavenly Father, help me let go of old ways of thinking and living. Renew my heart and mind to fully embrace the freedom of Jesus' promise that God forgives me and loves me. May I look at my world through the eyes of compassion, patience, and love. In Jesus' name I pray. Amen.

Prompts, Reflections, Actions

OBSERVE

- How did the scribes respond when Jesus forgave the sins of the paralyzed man?

- What do the old wineskins represent in the parable of the new wine and old wineskins?

- Why were the Pharisees and scribes upset that Jesus dined with tax collectors and sinners? How did Jesus respond to their criticism?

REFLECT

- If Jesus' truth is "new wine," how can you prepare yourself to carry that truth? If you're stuck in your old ways of thinking, how can you ask to be made new?

- Are you clinging to any attitudes or traditions that hinder you from fully embracing the freedom offered by Jesus' promise to us? If so, what are they?

APPLY

- What old ways of thinking and living can you let go of to make room to embrace the Gospel's message?

- Think of steps you can take to cultivate a new heart and mind.

Week Recap

Jesus shares a parable about new wine in old wineskins, symbolizing the need for new hearts to receive his Gospel message, which is incompatible with old traditions and ways of thinking and living. There may be patterns in our own life that are incompatible with the Gospel, but we can ask God to help renew our minds and replace these patterns.

*No one puts a piece of unshrunk cloth on an old garment;
for the patch pulls away from the garment, and the
tear is made worse. Nor do they put new wine into
old wineskins, or else the wineskins break, the wine is
spilled, and the wineskins are ruined. But they put new
wine into new wineskins, and both are preserved.*

MATTHEW 9:16–17 (NKJV)

DON'T LOSE HOPE

Reading Plan

DAY 1: John 5:1–9

DAY 2: John 5:10–13

DAY 3: John 5:14–18

DAY 4: John 5:19–30

DAY 5: John 5: 31–38

DAY 6: John 5: 39–47

DAY 7: Study and Reflection

Bible Study

In this week's readings, Jesus encounters a paralyzed man waiting for a miracle. Having suffered for 38 years, the man likely doubted whether he'd ever be healed. Can you relate? Sometimes we get accustomed to an unhealthy situation and give up hope of ever being restored. Or we may struggle with overcoming a destructive habit because the comfort and familiarity it gives us prevents us from fully wanting to be freed from it.

Or maybe you've felt desperate for a change, which has brought you to seek Jesus for healing. When we go through a tragedy or need a miracle in our life, we can seek hope in Jesus, who can help us overcome our insecurities, heal our deepest pain, transform our harmful thought patterns, and renew our minds.

When we experience a personal struggle, we may feel reluctant to seek Christ's help and healing. We may even feel resistant to admitting our weaknesses and need for God's help because we don't want to face them. Restoration begins with faith and a willingness to be healed. We can trust in him to transform our life no matter how long we have struggled with something, knowing that he is the one who can bring us true and lasting change.

Prayer

Dear heavenly Father, grow my desire for restoration in the parts of my life that need healing. Help me to loosen my grip on anything that separates me from you. Thank you for helping me to overcome my doubts and sins. In Jesus' name I pray. Amen.

Prompts, Reflections, Actions

OBSERVE

- What did Jesus say to the paralyzed man after healing him?

- How did Jesus respond to the Jewish leaders who accused him of breaking the Sabbath?

- What did Jesus say about his relationship with the Father?

REFLECT

- In what ways do you hold yourself back from seeking Christ's help and healing?

- Are there any patterns that God has asked you to distance yourself from?

- How do you normally respond in a situation that seems hopeless and impossible?

APPLY

- How can you overcome the doubt and hopelessness that come with prolonged suffering or difficult circumstances?

- Consider ways you can continue to trust and have faith in God's plan when you experience long-term trials or difficult situations, big or small, in life.

- How do you support your loved ones when they are experiencing doubt or hopelessness?

Week Recap

Jesus healed a man who had been paralyzed for 38 years. This story shows us that even when we give up hope in a situation or struggle with sin, we can turn to Jesus for help and healing. Those who believe in his power to heal can find a renewal of strength and hope.

Jesus saith unto him, Rise, take up thy bed, and walk. And immediately the man was made whole, and took up his bed, and walked: and on the same day was the sabbath.

JOHN 5:8–9 (KJV)

SEEING WHAT REALLY MATTERS

Reading Plan

DAY 1: Matthew 12:1–14

DAY 2: Matthew 12:15–21

DAY 3: Mark 2:23–28

DAY 4: Mark 3:1–12

DAY 5: Mark 3:13–19

DAY 6: Luke 6:1–16

DAY 7: Study and Reflection

Bible Study

In the passages for this week, the Pharisees are seen upholding man-made laws and traditions instead of prioritizing God's commandments. The Pharisees catch Jesus and his disciples walking through a field. The disciples are hungry, so they are picking grain and eating it as they go along. The Pharisees jump to accuse them of violating their strict interpretation of the law. They say the Sabbath was meant to be a day of rest, and here are Jesus' own disciples doing physical work by picking grain. Yes, the Sabbath was meant to be set aside for rest, but the Pharisees had added so many rules and restrictions that abiding by them all became an impossible burden, and the original intent of God's commandment was lost.

The Pharisees were so concerned with outward compliance to their laws that they disregarded the well-being of others and were blinded to the good that Jesus was doing. We can fall into the same trap, creating our own set of rules and regulations to be a "good" Christian. Doing that may help us feel like we are in control, but just like what happened to the Pharisees, it can cause us to lose sight of what really matters. We can go to church every Sunday, volunteer on every committee, and go through the motions of what we think it means to be "good." But if we aren't nurturing our personal relationship with Jesus and living a life that is guided by love, we will miss out on having God's heart for others.

Prayer

Dear heavenly Father, help me to remember that you look past
the motions we go through trying to be good. You see what's in
our hearts; help me to see others through your love. Help me
live a life that pleases you. In Jesus' name I pray. Amen.

Prompts, Reflections, Actions

OBSERVE

- In Luke 6, what did the Pharisees accuse Jesus' disciples of doing on the Sabbath?

- In Matthew 12, what Old Testament prophecy was fulfilled by Jesus' healing people?

- What did Jesus do to heal the man with the withered hand?

REFLECT

- Have you ever gone through the motions of being good, but your heart wasn't in it? How did that hinder your ability to show true compassion and care for others?

- Have you ever created rules or formulas about what makes a good Christian? How did that affect your relationship with God and others?

APPLY

- How can you avoid falling into the trap of self-righteousness when it comes to your faith?

- How can you follow Jesus' example of prioritizing the needs and well-being of others over strictly following established traditions?

Week Recap

The Pharisees' strict adherence to man-made laws over understanding God's heart behind his commandments is highlighted when they accuse Jesus and his disciples of violating the Sabbath. Their reaction shows a hardened, closed mindset that reflects pride and self-righteousness, causing them to miss God's heart for others and negating the original intent of his commandment.

And, behold, there was a man which had his hand withered. And they asked him, saying, Is it lawful to heal on the sabbath days? that they might accuse him. And he said unto them, What man shall there be among you, that shall have one sheep, and if it fall into a pit on the sabbath day, will he not lay hold on it, and lift it out?

MATTHEW 12:10–11 (KJV)

The Heart Matters Most

Reading Plan

DAY 1: Matthew 5:1–12

DAY 2: Matthew 5:13–20

DAY 3: Matthew 5:21–32

DAY 4: Matthew 5:33–48

DAY 5: Luke 6:17–26

DAY 6: Luke 6:27–36

DAY 7: Study and Reflection

Bible Study

Most of us at one time or another have acted a certain way to appear virtuous in front of others. We may experience a tension of feeling like we have to convey a picture-perfect image of ourselves. When we do this, we put on a mask or persona and don't show up authentically in our lives.

Jesus emphasizes the importance of acting from genuine love for God and others rather than striving to be seen as morally upright. God may point to areas of our life where we've been following a set of rules without deeply examining our hearts and motives. Jesus teaches in Matthew 5 that it's not enough to only obey the law or check off boxes to look righteous from the outside. The most important thing is to have a pure heart—not strive for external perfection. Having a pure heart allows us to draw closer to God and align our inner desires, thoughts, and actions with his heart.

When we ask God to help us to go deeper and examine our hearts, he can expose and remove any impure motives and areas of pride so that we can experience a transformation that is rooted in his love and led by his Spirit. This requires us to be fully honest, raw, and real with him and to take off any masks we may have put on to portray a perfect image of ourselves. Through this transformation, we can experience what it means to be truly righteous from within and reflect the heart of Jesus.

Prayer

Dear heavenly Father, I want to honor you in all that I do.
Help me to purify my heart so that my actions reflect the
love and grace of Christ. In Jesus' name I pray. Amen.

Prompts, Reflections, Actions

OBSERVE

- What did Jesus say about being "the salt of the earth" and "the light of the world"?

- How did Jesus say to behave toward your enemies and those who curse you?

- What does Matthew 5 say about communication?

REFLECT

- How do Jesus' teachings in this week's passages challenge your understanding of what it means to be a follower of Christ?

- Which beatitude do you find the most challenging to embody in your daily life?

APPLY

- Where do you struggle, and how can you support those areas with Jesus' teachings?

- How can you intentionally display love and kindness to those who can be difficult to love?

Week Recap

Jesus emphasizes that having a pure heart is more important than just following the law outwardly. He compares anger to murder and lust to adultery, highlighting the importance of our inner motives and desires. True righteousness is reflected within our heart, and Jesus challenges us to examine the motives of our hearts, not just our external behavior.

Blessed are the pure in heart: for they shall see God.

MATTHEW 5:8 (KJV)

OUR TREASURE IS IN HEAVEN

Reading Plan

DAY 1: Matthew 6:1–4

DAY 2: Matthew 6:5–15

DAY 3: Matthew 6:16–18

DAY 4: Matthew 6:19–24

DAY 5: Matthew 6:25–34

DAY 6: Luke 6:37–42

DAY 7: Study and Reflection

Bible Study

What do you value the most in your life? What do you worry about the most? In this week's readings, Jesus reminds us that our true treasure is in heaven and that we don't need to worry about whether our basic needs will be met. He reminds us that the birds of the air and the lilies of the field never worry, yet God provides everything they need. In Matthew 6, Jesus teaches us about the importance of putting our relationship with God ahead of worrying about our future. If we seek him first, we can trust that everything else will fall into place as he has intended. We can prioritize our relationship with God and make time to seek his guidance and align our actions with his will for us, knowing that we are in his loving and faithful hands. When we lose sight of this, we begin to devise our own plans and forget to include God in them; I can act as if I don't have a heavenly Father who knows what's best for me. It's easy to focus on everything going wrong, but we can fully trust in his provision and remember that he knows exactly what we need, even before we ask for it. We can experience contentment on Earth no matter what situation we are in, because we have the ultimate treasure of Jesus himself and eternal life in heaven with him.

Prayer

Dear heavenly Father, help me to seek your kingdom first and not worry about my future so I can focus on what's truly important: my relationship with you. In Jesus' name I pray. Amen.

Prompts, Reflections, Actions

OBSERVE

- What did Jesus say to seek first in Matthew 6?

- According to Matthew 6, what is the true treasure of a Christian?

- In Matthew 6, what did Jesus encourage his followers to do when it comes to worries about the future?

REFLECT

- What worries or fears do you struggle with the most?

- In what ways have you seen God provide for your needs in the past?

APPLY

- Commit to bringing every fear and worry to God in prayer. Ask him to help you trust in his provision and care for you, even in the midst of uncertainty.

- What might seeking God's kingdom first look like in practice throughout your daily life? Where can you make room to prioritize time with him and serving others?

Week Recap

We can seek heavenly treasures and prioritize our relationship with God above all else, confidently trusting that his love is always there, and that he knows what is best for us.

Lay not up for yourselves treasures upon earth, where
moth and rust doth corrupt, and where thieves break
through and steal: But lay up for yourselves treasures
in heaven, where neither moth nor rust doth corrupt,
and where thieves do not break through nor steal: For
where your treasure is, there will your heart be also.

MATTHEW 6:19-21 (KJV)

LIVING WITH INTEGRITY

Reading Plan

DAY 1: Matthew 7:1–6

DAY 2: Matthew 7:7–11

DAY 3: Matthew 7:12–14

DAY 4: Matthew 7:15–17

DAY 5: Matthew 7:18–20

DAY 6: Luke 6:43–45

DAY 7: Study and Reflection

Bible Study

In Matthew 7, Jesus teaches about the dangers of hypocrisy. He illustrates this lesson by suggesting that hypocrites attempt to remove a speck of dust from someone else's eye while ignoring the giant plank in their own. Today, it can look like pretending to be something we're not, saying one thing but doing another. It might also look like responding defensively to constructive feedback and pointing out flaws in others or refusing to acknowledge our role or responsibility for our actions. Have you ever noticed yourself being severely judgmental of someone and realizing what you were criticizing was really something you didn't like about yourself? Sometimes we notice things about others that, deep down inside, we dislike about ourselves. But instead of working on our own shortcomings, it's easier to point our finger elsewhere.

Jesus taught that we should not judge others before examining ourselves and recognizing our own faults. So, step 1 is acknowledging our own weaknesses. Rather than being critical of flaws in others, we can ask God for help to overcome our own. We can learn to be more intentional about examining our motives and checking to see that our words and actions align with our beliefs. As we strive to live a life free from hypocrisy, we can trust that God will guide and empower us to live authentically and honestly.

Prayer

Dear heavenly Father, help me to avoid the pitfalls of hypocrisy and work toward overcoming my faults. Help me align my motives and actions with your will. In Jesus' name I pray. Amen.

Prompts, Reflections, Actions

OBSERVE

- What did Jesus warn against in Matthew 7:1–5?

- In Matthew 7:12, what is the "golden rule" that Jesus taught?

- According to Matthew 7:15–20, how can you recognize a "false prophet" or deceptive person who claims to speak for God?

REFLECT

- When have you judged others before examining yourself? How did that impact your relationships?

- How does being more aware of your own faults and weaknesses impact your relationship with God and others?

APPLY

- Where can you add more mindful examination in your motives and intentions before acting?

- In what ways can you practice humility and avoid the trap of wanting to appear righteous in front of others?

Week Recap

Jesus urges us to first examine ourselves before judging others. Hypocrisy creates a barrier between us and God, but we can overcome it by acknowledging our faults, relying on the Holy Spirit to live out our faith consistently, and asking God for help to overcome our weaknesses.

Judge not, that you be not judged. For with what judgment you judge, you will be judged; and with the measure you use, it will be measured back to you. And why do you look at the speck in your brother's eye, but do not consider the plank in your own eye? Or how can you say to your brother, 'Let me remove the speck from your eye'; and look, a plank is in your own eye?

MATTHEW 7:1-4 (NKJV)

BUILD YOUR HOUSE ON ROCK, NOT SAND

Reading Plan

DAY 1: Matthew 7:21-23

DAY 2: Matthew 7:24-29

DAY 3: Matthew 8:5-13

DAY 4: Luke 6:46-49

DAY 5: Luke 7:1-10

DAY 6: Luke 7:11-17

DAY 7: Study and Reflection

Bible Study

Matthew 7 describes a parable about two builders—one wise and one foolish—to illustrate the importance of building our lives on a solid foundation. One way we build our house on shaky ground is by basing our worth on temporary things, such as worldly pursuits, relationships, our body image, or career aspirations. One way to know if we've done this is to ask ourselves, "What if we no longer had our worldly possessions, status, or relationships? Would we be OK without them?" Apart from God, whatever we think we cannot live without is something that has become a god in our life—an idol.

But when we build our identity around Jesus, we know we are loved, accepted, and complete in him and that our future is secure. Basing our identity on Jesus means we can weather any storm with faith, peace, and hope, knowing that there is no foundation more secure than Jesus to build our life upon! Even when unexpected trials arise, the entire foundation will remain intact. Jesus is the same yesterday, today, and forever (Hebrews 13:8). He has freed us from worrying about what others think of us or tying our worth to our social status or what's in our bank account. As we prioritize our relationship with God and build our house on rock, we can experience a peace and purpose that go beyond the short-lived pleasures and troubles of this world.

Prayer

Dear heavenly Father, build my life on a solid foundation of faith in you. May I prioritize my relationship with you and apply your teachings in my daily life. In Jesus' name I pray. Amen.

Prompts, Reflections, Actions

OBSERVE

- What happened to the house built on sand?

- Whom did Jesus consider a wise man?

- How did people respond to the parable of the two builders?

REFLECT

- What does it mean to you to base your identity and worth in Jesus?

- Have you ever experienced a time when your faith was shaken because of a storm in your life? What did you turn to first?

- Recall a time in which you felt secure and peaceful while experiencing God's presence despite uncertain times.

APPLY

- What aspects of your identity have you built that are based on the temporary things of this world? How might you rebuild them on a solid foundation?

- What actionable steps can you take to prioritize your relationship with God?

Week Recap

In Matthew 7, Jesus shares a parable about building our lives on a solid foundation. When we depend on Jesus and prioritize our relationship with God, we can weather the storms of life and experience a sense of peace and purpose that transcends worldly pleasures and troubles.

Therefore whosoever heareth these sayings of mine, and doeth them, I will liken him unto a wise man, which built his house upon a rock: And the rain descended, and the floods came, and the winds blew, and beat upon that house; and it fell not: for it was founded upon a rock.

MATTHEW 7:24–25 (KJV)

Unburdened by Jesus' Yoke

Reading Plan

DAY 1: Matthew 11:1-19

DAY 2: Matthew 11:20-30

DAY 3: Luke 7:18-35

DAY 4: Luke 7:36-50

DAY 5: Matthew 12:22-37

DAY 6: Mark 3:20-30

DAY 7: Study and Reflection

Bible Study

A yoke, the wooden beam used to connect two animals to plow fields or pull carts, is a symbol of hard work. Jesus offers a different kind of yoke—one that provides rest and peace.

Jesus' yoke is easy because he is not asking us to work for our salvation or earn his love. Instead, he invites us to trust him and follow his example. Jesus knows that life can be burdensome and overwhelming at times, and he promises to walk alongside us. He not only leads us where to go but also helps us carry our load. We often overlook this invitation. We may feel that we would burden or annoy Jesus with all our problems. We may believe that if we just hustle and grind and carry the load ourselves, we can earn and deserve the good things in life.

Rather than taking Jesus' yoke, we may have yoked ourselves to things or relationships that influence us away from him. But Jesus' yoke is perfect. He takes the weight of our sin and our struggles upon himself when we simply choose to accept his help. Jesus is asking you to give him the burdens and challenges, no matter how big or small, that you may be facing.

To rest in him and take on his yoke, we must surrender our own desires and plans to him, let him lead us, and unburden all our cares and worries onto him.

Prayer

Dear heavenly Father, thank you for offering me rest and ease through Jesus' yoke. Help me to trust in him and find complete rest for my soul. In Jesus' name I pray. Amen.

Prompts, Reflections, Actions

OBSERVE

- Who was asking Jesus the questions in Matthew 11?

- When the crowd asked Jesus about John the Baptist, how did he reply?

- In Matthew 11:25–27, what did Jesus reveal about the Father and the Son?

REFLECT

- What burdens that you currently carry are weighing you down?

- What areas of your life are you struggling to surrender to Jesus' control?

APPLY

- How can you actively seek rest in Jesus in the midst of a busy and demanding day?

- How can you approach work and responsibilities with peace and purpose?

Week Recap

In Matthew 11, Jesus invites us to take on his easy yoke, which provides rest and peace. His yoke is not a burden, because he takes our struggles and sins upon himself. Surrendering our troubles and worries to him, we can find rest by reading his Word, learning from his example, and reminding ourselves we're never alone.

> *Come unto me, all ye that labour and are heavy laden, and*
> *I will give you rest. Take my yoke upon you, and learn of me;*
> *for I am meek and lowly in heart: and ye shall find rest unto*
> *your souls. For my yoke is easy, and my burden is light.*
>
> MATTHEW 11:28–30 (KJV)

Rooted in God's Word

Reading Plan

DAY 1: Matthew 12:38–50

DAY 2: Matthew 13:1–9

DAY 3: Matthew 13:10–23

DAY 4: Luke 8:1–21

DAY 5: Mark 3:31–35

DAY 6: Mark 4:1–25

DAY 7: Study and Reflection

Bible Study

In Matthew 13, we see Jesus telling a parable about a farmer sowing seeds on four types of soil: the path, the rocky ground, the thorns, and the good soil. Seeds on the path are eaten by birds, those on rocky ground sprout quickly but wither away, and those among the thorns are choked out. But the ones sowed on good soil bear fruit.

This parable is usually discussed as an analogy to describe different kinds of hearts that receive God's Word. However, the soil in our own hearts may also respond differently to God's Word depending on the season of our life. Sometimes our heart may be hardened or closed off from receiving God's Word when we become complacent in our walk. Cultivating good soil in our hearts looks like allowing the Word of God to take root in our hearts. Challenges in life have the potential to hinder our spiritual growth. Do we get too busy to spend intentional time each day reading and meditating on the Bible? Do we pray before moving about our day? Do we take time for personal reflection and open our hearts to receive what God might have for us in his Word? Or do we avoid it and distract ourselves from it?

Cultivating fertile ground for God's Word in our hearts means regularly nurturing our faith and continuing to work toward aligning our hearts with the values that God instills in us. Through this, we can experience the abundant life and fruitfulness that Jesus promised to those who hear his message.

Prayer

Dear heavenly Father, help me to have ears that hear and a heart that understands your truth. May I cultivate fertile soil for your Word to take root and bear fruit in my life. In Jesus' name I pray. Amen.

Prompts, Reflections, Actions

OBSERVE

- What does the seed represent in the parable of the sower?

- What do the four types of soil represent?

- What is significant about the seed that falls on fertile soil?

- Which type of soil best describes your heart's current condition toward God's Word?

- What distractions or worries obstruct your faith?

APPLY

• What would deepening your roots in God's Word look like to you?

• Think of some ways God's Word can cultivate and nurture your relationships this week.

Week Recap

In Matthew 13, Jesus teaches a parable about a farmer sowing seeds on different types of soil. The condition of our hearts determines how we receive and nurture God's Word. We can work to cultivate fertile ground and experience the abundant life and spiritual fruitfulness Jesus promised.

*But he that received seed into the good ground is
he that heareth the word, and understandeth it;
which also beareth fruit, and bringeth forth, some
an hundredfold, some sixty, some thirty.*

MATTHEW 13:23 (KJV)

MUSTARD SEED FAITH

Reading Plan

DAY 1: Matthew 13:24–30

DAY 2: Matthew 13:31–35

DAY 3: Mark 4:26–29

DAY 4: Mark 4:30–34

DAY 5: Matthew 9:18–34

DAY 6: Matthew 9:35–38

DAY 7: Study and Reflection

Bible Study

Just as a tiny mustard seed grows into a large bush, our faith can grow from a small beginning and flourish over time as we nurture it with prayer, reading the Bible, and trusting in God's promises.

There have been many times when God showed up unexpectedly even with a tiny amount of faith on my part. Even when our faith deepens and matures, we encounter certain seasons over time, and it's hard to be full of faith. At times like those, I remind myself that a mustard seed–sized faith is all I need, and I begin there, knowing that God is ever faithful and never fails.

As God builds our faith, it will be tested—when we feel disappointment or question God's plan and purpose for our lives, face hard decisions, or are in the midst of one of life's storms or a season of grieving. These trials are an opportunity for us to step out in faith and for God to surprise us, secure us in the knowledge of his love for us, and show us that he has a plan for our lives. We may not always see God's plan or understand his ways, but we can trust that he is working all things together for our good.

Prayer

Dear heavenly Father, help my mustard seed faith to grow greater every day. Strengthen my conviction and help me to trust in your plan. I know that you can move mountains! In Jesus' name I pray. Amen.

Prompts, Reflections, Actions

OBSERVE

- What did Jesus compare the kingdom of God to?

- What did Jesus say would happen to those who had the ears to hear?

- What happened to the mustard seed when it was sowed?

REFLECT

- What can the mustard seed teach you about patience and perseverance in your own faith journey?

- Have you ever experienced God revealing his hand after a small act of faith?

APPLY

- What can you do to cultivate an attitude of patience and perseverance in your faith journey?

- What is one area of your life where you can ask for God's help this week to grow and transform you?

Week Recap

Jesus teaches about the mustard seed, a very small seed, which grows into the largest plant in the garden. This parable reminds us that even the smallest acts of faith can grow into something great when nurtured by God. Trust in God's power to bring about big changes from small beginnings.

Another parable put he forth unto them, saying, The kingdom of heaven is like to a grain of mustard seed, which a man took, and sowed in his field: Which indeed is the least of all seeds: but when it is grown, it is the greatest among herbs, and becometh a tree, so that the birds of the air come and lodge in the branches thereof.

MATTHEW 13:31–32 (KJV)

WEEK 20

THE PRICELESS
PEARL

Reading Plan

DAY 1: Matthew 13:33–35

DAY 2: Matthew 13:36–43

DAY 3: Matthew 13:44–46

DAY 4: Matthew 13:47–50

DAY 5: Matthew 13:51–52

DAY 6: Matthew 13:53–58

DAY 7: Study and Reflection

Bible Study

When you think of what you treasure most in your life, what comes out on top? Like the merchant in the parable of the finest pearls, when we find the joy of Jesus' message and cherish it, we are motivated to release anything that moves us away from God. When we find what matters most, we clear away the clutter in our lives and make room for God to enter and fill us up.

Once I began to take small steps to prioritize God and my relationship with him despite the demands of everyday life, I started to see how much I needed him. My eyes were opened to how much fuller my life was when I walked closely with him. And although there are times I don't feel like attending church or a Bible study, I now treasure my time with him, knowing that the time soaking in his Word is like oxygen to me and that I need it to sustain me throughout the rest of my week.

Prayer

Dear heavenly Father, guide me in recognizing the value of your kingdom above all else. Give me the strength to make the necessary sacrifices to bring glory to your kingdom. In Jesus' name I pray. Amen.

Prompts, Reflections, Actions

OBSERVE

- What does the pearl represent in the parable?

- What sacrifice did the merchant make to possess the pearl?

- How does the value of the pearl in the parable compare to other pearls in the merchant's collection?

REFLECT

- Have you been as excited about seeking the kingdom of God as the merchant seeking the valuable pearl?

- Would you be willing to give up everything for God's kingdom if needed?

- In what ways does the world distract you from seeking the kingdom of God?

APPLY

- This week, find moments to savor and cherish where God is actively working in your daily life.

- What actions and habits can you start to cultivate to pursue God more fully in your life?

Week Recap

The parable of the valuable pearl emphasizes the worth of God's kingdom and the sacrifice required to obtain it. We must be willing to let go of anything that hinders us from pursuing God's kingdom wholeheartedly, remembering that Jesus paid the ultimate sacrifice for us to inherit eternal life.

> *Again, the kingdom of heaven is like unto a merchant man,*
> *seeking goodly pearls: Who, when he had found one pearl*
> *of great price, went and sold all that he had, and bought it.*

MATTHEW 13:45–46 (KJV)

Finding Peace in the Storm

Reading Plan

DAY 1: Matthew 8:18–34

DAY 2: Matthew 9:18–38

DAY 3: Mark 4:35–41; Mark 5:1–20

DAY 4: Mark 5:21–43

DAY 5: Luke 8:22–39

DAY 6: Luke 8:40–56

DAY 7: Study and Reflection

Bible Study

In this week's passages, Jesus demonstrates his unlimited power time and time again, from driving out demons to healing and even raising a woman from the dead. However, when a storm arises, the disciples doubt Jesus even though they had previously witnessed his power.

Even if we've experienced God's ability to meet our needs, we may still question whether he cares for us in our present circumstances. When we don't see anything changing in our relationships, our financial situation, or our health, we might wonder why God doesn't seem to take any action. Sometimes we may even question whether we brought on the storm ourselves because of something we did wrong.

While storms test our faith, Jesus will help us make it through—just like he did with the disciples. Feeling his presence with us can help us remain calm even in the middle of turmoil. We're human, so it's natural to feel fear at times. But we can also have faith in God's promise that he's right there with us in the storm. Knowing we'll never be alone can give us the confidence to withstand any trouble that comes our way.

Prayer

Dear heavenly Father, you calm the storms and still the waves in the sea of my life—and when storms rage, you calm me. Help me to trust in your unlimited power even in the roughest parts of life. In Jesus' name I pray. Amen.

Prompts, Reflections, Actions

OBSERVE

- How did the disciples react during the storm?

- What was Jesus doing during the storm?

- How did Jesus respond to the disciples' reaction to the storm?

REFLECT

- Have you ever questioned God's presence and care for you? How did you get through those times?

- Think of a time when you experienced God demonstrate his power in your life. How can that memory help you face future storms?

- How does it feel to know you'll never be alone in a storm?

APPLY

- Remind yourself of God's power by jotting down all the good things that he does in your life to encourage you when the storms of life hit. If this isn't something you're already doing, you can start today! Recall some events from your life where God carried you through a storm.

- What practical steps can you take to deepen your faith so that you're more prepared for the storms of life?

Week Recap

This week focused on how storms can test our faith and illustrated Jesus' power over all creation. God's promise to be with us through every difficult circumstance reassures us that we can withstand any trouble that comes our way.

And he arose, and rebuked the wind, and said unto the sea, Peace, be still. And the wind ceased, and there was a great calm. And he said unto them, Why are ye so fearful? how is it that ye have no faith? And they feared exceedingly, and said one to another, What manner of man is this, that even the wind and the sea obey him?

MARK 4:39–41 (KJV)

SATISFIED

Reading Plan

DAY 1: Matthew 10:1–42

DAY 2: Matthew 14:1–36

DAY 3: Mark 6:1–56

DAY 4: Luke 9:1–24

DAY 5: John 6:1–34

DAY 6: John 6:35–49

DAY 7: Study and Reflection

Bible Study

The miracle of the loaves and fishes is a wonderful reminder of how Jesus equips us and provides for our needs. A huge crowd had gathered to hear Jesus teach, and when the day grew late and people began to get hungry, Jesus responded by using the few loaves and fish that were available to perform a miracle and satisfy the people's needs.

We all want to feel comfortable and secure in our lives. Sometimes we get fixated on making sure our pantry is stocked, thinking that having enough will keep us happy. But obsessing over our earthly wants and needs distracts us from the calling God has for us: to set aside our temporary comfort and first seek our life in him. When we answer that call, he equips and empowers us to bless others. When we are committed to following Jesus, he will meet our most important spiritual needs. We don't need to be afraid to step out in faith, because we can trust in his provision, knowing that he cares for us more than we can ever imagine.

Prayer

Dear heavenly Father, help me to trust in your provision
and seek to find my life in you rather than the things
of this world. In Jesus' name I pray. Amen.

Prompts, Reflections, Actions

OBSERVE

- What did Jesus say about people who are willing to lose their life?

- In Luke 9, what did Jesus say after Peter declared that Jesus was the Messiah?

- How did Jesus meet his disciples who were in a boat in the middle of the sea?

REFLECT

- Jesus said that he is the "bread of life." What does that mean to you?

- In what ways has God met your physical and spiritual needs?

APPLY

- Are there ways that you have prioritized your physical desires over your spiritual needs? What are some steps you can take to ensure that you are spiritually fed?

- Think about special gifts that God has equipped you with. How do you use those special gifts to bless others and share God's love with those around you?

Week Recap

This week's devotion reminds us that God calls us to seek him, not just to fulfill our earthly desires. We can trust that God will provide for us and equip us to serve others. We can overcome our fear with faith, which allows us to receive God's blessings far beyond having our physical needs met.

> *Then he took the five loaves and the two fishes, and looking up to heaven, he blessed them, and brake, and gave to the disciples to set before the multitude. And they did eat, and were all filled: and there was taken up of fragments that remained to them twelve baskets.*

LUKE 9:16–17 (KJV)

SEASONS OF WAITING

Reading Plan

DAY 1: Matthew 15:1-20

DAY 2: Matthew 15:21-39

DAY 3: Matthew 16:1-12

DAY 4: Mark 7:1-37

DAY 5: Mark 8:1-26

DAY 6: John 6:50-64

DAY 7: Study and Reflection

Bible Study

Have you ever experienced what seemed like silence from God? Perhaps you prayed about something but didn't hear God's answer or felt alone, unable to sense his presence. In Matthew 15, we read the story of a Canaanite woman who, despite being met with silence, persists in her plea for Jesus to deliver her suffering daughter from a demon.

Jesus responds to the woman's perseverance by commending her great faith and instantly heals her daughter from a distance. Despite her struggle, the woman's relentless faith and dependence on Jesus serves as an example of what to do even when we do not receive an immediate answer to our prayers.

Seasons of waiting can be challenging to our faith, and it's tempting to give up on God when we don't see any immediate change in our situation. Maybe you've been in a waiting period of singleness or transitioning in your career. Our natural response is to try to take matters into our own hands when things don't get settled as quickly as we'd like. But times such as these can draw out our faith and strengthen it as we continue to turn to God and wait with faith on his perfect timing.

Prayer

Dear heavenly Father, help me to persist in my faith and trust
in your timing. Please bless and provide healing for others
who need and seek you. In Jesus' name I pray. Amen.

Prompts, Reflections, Actions

OBSERVE

- How did Jesus first respond to the Canaanite woman's request for help?

- How did the disciples want Jesus to respond to the woman?

- What was Jesus' final response to the Canaanite woman's request for healing?

REFLECT

- Can you relate to the Canaanite woman's feelings? How might her persistence translate to your own faith?

- Have there been times when you've felt like God hasn't been hearing your prayers? How did you deal with that, and what was the outcome?

APPLY

- This week's readings showed that silence from God does not mean he is ignoring your prayer. What would you like to plan to do the next time you experience his silence?

- Take a moment to pray for healing for others who are struggling.

- In what ways can you trust in God's love and compassion, even when circumstances seem to be against you? What helps you hold on and wait on God's timing?

Week Recap

God does not always immediately answer our prayers. But that does not mean he doesn't plan to answer them at all. Even when the odds seem stacked against us, we can remember that God has compassion for all those who need his help, and we can be persistent in prayer.

Then Jesus answered and said unto her, O woman,
great is thy faith: be it unto thee even as thou wilt. And
her daughter was made whole from that very hour.

MATTHEW 15:28 (KJV)

True Greatness in God's Kingdom

Reading Plan

DAY 1: Matthew 16:13–28

DAY 2: Matthew 17:1–27

DAY 3: Matthew 18:1–35

DAY 4: Mark 8:27–38

DAY 5: Mark 9:1–50

DAY 6: Luke 9:25–62

DAY 7: Study and Reflection

Bible Study

What does "greatness" mean to you? Having an organized home, an impressive career, perfect children? In today's world, the idea of greatness is often equated with wealth, power, and status. But in God's kingdom, greatness is measured by our humility and willingness to serve others, as Jesus explains in Luke 9:46–48 and Mark 9:33–37. In God's way of thinking, the least are the greatest.

Striving for greatness in God's kingdom looks like walking in his will, overcoming our tendency for self-centeredness, and being quick to forgive others even when it's challenging. Rather than striving to be sufficient by our own strength, we can humbly accept God's mercy, grace, and forgiveness.

When we're busy and absorbed in our own cares, it can be easy to miss out on opportunities to bless others. But if we want to attain the kind of greatness God values, we can start by caring for others' souls the way he cares so deeply for ours and fulfill our highest calling in our life, which is to serve others through his power.

Prayer

Dear heavenly Father, help me to follow you with a heart to serve, and inspire me to forgive as you did. May I live for your glory rather than my own. In Jesus' name I pray. Amen.

Prompts, Reflections, Actions

OBSERVE

- In Matthew 18, what did Jesus teach about forgiveness?

- What does Mark 8 reveal about the value of our soul?

- In Mark 9:33–37, what did Jesus say about greatness in the kingdom of God?

REFLECT

- In what ways does the world's definition of greatness differ from God's definition of greatness?

- God reminds us to be in partnership with him as we pursue our ambitions, not prioritizing our goals above his will for our lives. What gifts and talents has God given you? How are those gifts and talents used to bless others?

APPLY

- In what ways do you bless and care for others as God cares for you?

- How can you cultivate a heart that desires to follow God?

- When you prioritize your spiritual growth, how different does your typical day look?

Week Recap

In God's kingdom, greatness is defined by humility and a willingness to serve others just as Jesus did. That means that if we would strive for greatness, we must learn to value forgiving others, looking for ways to help, and letting go of our pride. God values our dedication to him and others more than anything in this world and calls us to care for others just as he does.

And Jesus, perceiving the thought of their heart, took a child, and set him by him, And said unto them, Whosoever shall receive this child in my name receiveth me: and whosoever shall receive me receiveth him that sent me: for he that is least among you all, the same shall be great.

LUKE 9:47–48 (KJV)

Freedom from Condemnation

Reading Plan

DAY 1: John 6:65–71

DAY 2: John 7:1–13

DAY 3: John 7:14–24

DAY 4: John 7:25–44

DAY 5: John 7:45–53

DAY 6: John 8:1–11

DAY 7: Study and Reflection

Bible Study

In John 8, a group of Pharisees try to trap Jesus in a difficult situation by accusing a woman of adultery, thinking the woman would have to be stoned or Jesus would spare her and break God's sacred law. In response, Jesus doesn't deny the law, nor does he condone the woman's sin. Instead, he exposes the Pharisees' hypocrisy by telling them that whichever of them is without sin is welcome to cast the first stone. When each of the accusers leaves, Jesus turns to the woman and tells her that he does not condemn her and that she should no longer sin.

Have you ever felt unforgivable? Like you've committed a sin so great that you feel unworthy of pardon? Let the story in John 8 remind you that Jesus did not come to condemn us but came to save us (John 3:16–17). Jesus drew near the woman in spite of her reputation and wrongdoing and embraced her, freeing her from shame and giving her an opportunity to transform.

No matter how much we've sinned in the past, God is quick to forgive and does not want us to define ourselves by it. It can feel challenging to accept God's mercy. But when we truly understand his unconditional love and desire for our freedom, we can be empowered to wholeheartedly accept forgiveness and move forward, strengthened to resist the temptation of sin in the future and no longer live under condemnation.

Prayer

Dear heavenly Father, thank you for sending Jesus to save me from my sins. Help me to see the balance between your grace and truth and to live a better life. In Jesus' name I pray. Amen.

Prompts, Reflections, Actions

OBSERVE

- How did Jesus respond when the Pharisees asked him about stoning the woman?

- How did Jesus expose the hypocrisy of the Pharisees in John 8:1–11?

- What did Jesus tell the woman caught in adultery after he had forgiven her and saved her from being stoned?

REFLECT

- Have you ever experienced both the truth that you're not perfect and the grace that you're forgiven in your life? How has that impacted your relationship with God and others?

- Have you ever felt condemned because of your own mistakes? How can Jesus' response to the woman in John 8 offer you hope and freedom?

APPLY

- Are there areas of your life where you are holding onto guilt or shame over past mistakes or sins? How can you absorb Jesus' words in John 8:11 into your own life and invite freedom and healing?

- How can you apply the lesson of John 8 to your interactions with others who may be struggling?

Week Recap

In John 8, the Pharisees tried to trap Jesus by presenting a woman caught committing adultery. Jesus exposed their hypocrisy and taught about mercy and freedom from sin. He came not to condemn us but to save us, and knowing that we are loved and forgiven in spite of our past empowers us to resist temptation.

*When Jesus had lifted up himself, and saw none
but the woman, he said unto her, Woman, where are
those thine accusers? hath no man condemned thee?
She said, No man, Lord. And Jesus said unto her,
Neither do I condemn thee: go, and sin no more.*

JOHN 8:10–11 (KJV)

Finding Purpose in Our Pain

Reading Plan

DAY 1: John 8:12–20

DAY 2: John 8:21–30

DAY 3: John 8:31–47

DAY 4: John 8:48–59

DAY 5: John 9:1–12

DAY 6: John 9:13–23

DAY 7: Study and Reflection

Bible Study

Maybe like the man who was born blind in John 9, you've dealt with a challenging physical issue, or perhaps you've experienced emotional pain that's left you feeling defeated and broken. In this week's reading from John, the disciples try to explain away the man's blindness by blaming him or his parents for his condition. But Jesus quickly corrects their misconceptions and heals the man in a very unusual way.

You may have experienced God's healing in mysterious ways in your own life like I have. In my healing journey, I've had to rely on Jesus' power to help me overcome deep emotional wounds from my past. There were times when all I wanted was a quick fix to resolve my pain. And sometimes I coped with it by blaming other people or circumstances for my difficulties. But when I relied on Jesus to pull me out, he transformed me and freed me, leading me to seek a deeper purpose to my life and transforming what I learned from my pain to be used purposefully and meaningfully to serve others.

Prayer

Dear heavenly Father, thank you for being the light in my darkness and healing me from my pain. Open my eyes to your purpose for my life and help me to trust in you alone. In Jesus' name I pray. Amen.

Prompts, Reflections, Actions

OBSERVE

- What did Jesus say would lead to freedom in John 8:32?

- What was the reason Jesus gave for the man's blindness at birth in John 9:3?

- How did the Pharisees react to the healing of the blind man in John 9:13–23?

REFLECT

- Have you seen God work in mysterious and unexpected ways in your life? List a few.

- How has God used your limitations to lead you to him? Or how have your limitations caused you to rely more on God?

- In what ways can you share God's love with those who may be experiencing pain or hardship?

- This week, reflect on one way God has brought healing and purpose for your life from a dark season you've experienced.

Week Recap

Pain can leave us feeling defeated, but God can heal us in unexpected ways and open our eyes to his purpose for our lives. In our moments of need, we can learn to rely on him and him alone.

When He had said these things, He spat on the ground and made clay with the saliva; and He anointed the eyes of the blind man with the clay. And He said to him, "Go, wash in the pool of Siloam" (which is translated, Sent). So he went and washed, and came back seeing.

JOHN 9:6–7 (NKJV)

HEARING GOD'S VOICE ABOVE THE NOISE

Reading Plan

DAY 1: John 9:24–41

DAY 2: John 10:1–10

DAY 3: John 10:11–21

DAY 4: John 10:22–30

DAY 5: John 10:31–42

DAY 6: Luke 10:1–16

DAY 7: Study and Reflection

Bible Study

With the noise of different voices in this world, we're constantly being pulled in multiple directions at once. The voices of our culture, family members, coworkers, and friends may be very loud and contradict one another. Wouldn't it be nice to know for sure which way to go? When we choose to trust God, we can begin to discern his voice from the world's distractions. Our Shepherd calls each of his sheep by name and desires us to develop a loving relationship with him. We can learn to hear our true Shepherd's voice by spending time with him through prayer and meditation on his Word.

Even when we feel trapped by the struggles of life or weighed down by our failures, God knows every one of his sheep's deepest needs. He laid down his life for us so that we could have a life abundant with his peace, grace, and mercy. When we're challenged by a decision or led into unfamiliar territory, we can trust God to take us on the right path and feel secure in his hands. When we are open to hearing and knowing God's voice, we can personally encounter his perfect love.

Prayer

Dear heavenly Father, please help me to discern your voice above all others. Teach me to trust and follow you, knowing that you will lead me to abundant life. In Jesus' name I pray. Amen.

Prompts, Reflections, Actions

OBSERVE

- What did Jesus say about the enemy in John 10:10?

- How did Jesus describe his relationship with the Father in John 10?

- What promise did Jesus give to his sheep in John 10:28?

REFLECT

- How have you experienced the guidance and protection of Jesus?

- In what ways have you struggled to discern God's voice through the noise of the world?

APPLY

- In what areas of your life do you struggle to trust where God is leading you? What areas would you like to surrender to him and his plan?

- What would committing to spend more time in God's presence this week look like for you? List a few simple ways to incorporate him into your days this week.

- What distractions are pulling you away from following Jesus? How can you actively choose to follow him instead?

Week Recap

John 10 presents Jesus as the good shepherd who knows and loves his sheep. He leads them on the right path, he gives them abundant life, and no one can take them out of his care. Jesus is also the door to salvation, and those who follow him can learn to discern and trust his voice.

My sheep hear my voice, and I know them, and they follow me: And I give unto them eternal life; and they shall never perish, neither shall any man pluck them out of my hand.

JOHN 10:27–28 (KJV)

SERVE FROM LOVE

Reading Plan

DAY 1: Luke 10:17–24

DAY 2: Luke 10:25–42

DAY 3: Luke 11:1–13

DAY 4: Luke 11:14–28

DAY 5: Luke 11:29–44

DAY 6: Luke 11:45–54

DAY 7: Study and Reflection

Bible Study

Are there times you've been so busy that it's hard to stop and rest at the feet of Jesus? We get so worried about our endless to-do lists and become resentful toward those who aren't helping us. We might even begin to feel self-righteous about our hard efforts—especially when others don't seem to be pulling their weight. Like Martha in this week's reading, we can become so focused on getting things done that we overemphasize outward appearances and lose sight of the most important priority in our life. When we work without taking time to connect with Jesus, we will serve from a disconnected heart. Our desire to be seen as a good servant becomes our motive rather than an earnest desire to help.

All of that changes when our motivation to serve flows from an out-pouring of God's love—and the best way to experience that is by sitting at Jesus' feet and receiving it, like Mary did. In certain seasons, it might be difficult to find the time to sit with Jesus and be filled with the Spirit so that we can serve from love, but we can ask him for wisdom on how to use our time effectively. We can have his peace in our hearts instead of being anxious and fretful about doing everything perfectly. And then, restored and recharged, we can face our to-do list from a place of abundant overflow.

Prayer

Dear heavenly Father, help me prioritize time spent at your feet. May my service flow from a heart that is connected to you and motivated by your love. In Jesus' name I pray. Amen.

Prompts, Reflections, Actions

OBSERVE

- What was Martha busy doing?

- Why was Martha upset?

- What was the good thing that Martha missed but Mary was present for?

REFLECT

- What hinders you from prioritizing your time spent with God?

- Do you relate more to Martha or to Mary? Can you think of a time when you emphasized outward appearances while serving God or a time when you were able to rest at Jesus' feet even though there were other things to do? How might you shift your motivation and still be of service?

- Do you tend to serve from a place of love or strictly because you feel an obligation? What is the result in each case?

APPLY

- What are some practical ways you can prioritize putting Jesus at the center of your days and schedule?

- How can you cultivate the habit of asking God for wisdom on how to spend your time effectively, especially during busy seasons?

Week Recap

This week's devotion highlights the importance of prioritizing time at Jesus' feet amid the busyness of life. Our service should flow from a heart that puts Jesus at the center, and our motivation to serve should reflect an outpouring of his love through us.

And Jesus answered and said unto her, Martha, Martha, thou art careful and troubled about many things: But one thing is needful: and Mary hath chosen that good part, which shall not be taken away from her.

LUKE 10:41–42 (KJV)

Invest in Eternity

Reading Plan

DAY 1: Luke 12:1–12

DAY 2: Luke 12:13–31

DAY 3: Luke 12:32–48

DAY 4: Luke 12:49–59

DAY 5: Luke 13:1–13

DAY 6: Luke 13:14–22

DAY 7: Study and Reflection

Bible Study

In this week's readings, we hear Jesus say that it is foolish to focus on accumulating earthly possessions for ourselves but not on being rich in our relationship with God. When we are too fixated on what we have, we'll be bound to living for it, in constant fear of losing it.

It's natural to sometimes buzz with the worries and fears of this life. We may wonder how we're going to pay our bills, make good grades, heal from heartbreak, grieve a loss, or overcome a health challenge. As a result, we work hard to achieve a certain level of stability in our lives, to "have it all," thinking that security somehow lies in the accumulation of worldly goods and achievements.

But God asks us to value what's eternal and trust him to provide for us as a good Father who cherishes his children. We can be relieved of the burdens we carry by investing our hearts in God's eternity, by pursuing his kingdom and setting our sights on heaven. We can work toward this by showing love, gratitude, generosity, kindness, and goodness in our daily lives and sharing the Gospel with others. Instead of focusing on what makes us rich here, we can focus on what makes us rich in eternity.

Prayer

Dear heavenly Father, please help me to focus on what's eternal and not be distracted by the world's desires. Teach me to trust in you as a good Father who provides for me. In Jesus' name I pray. Amen.

Prompts, Reflections, Actions

OBSERVE

- In Luke 12:6–7, what reason did Jesus give that we shouldn't give in to our fear?

- In Luke 12:15, what was Jesus' warning about greed?

- In Luke 12:31, Jesus said seeking the kingdom of God should be our top priority. What did he say will happen when we do that?

REFLECT

- Has there ever been a time when you put your trust in money and possessions?

- Have you ever struggled with coveting what is not yours?

- Recall a time when you felt fulfilled and satisfied with what you had. How did you give thanks to God for the blessings?

APPLY

- How can we remind ourselves to give thanks to God for the blessings in our lives?

- How can you build trust in God as your good Father and provider— and how might you respond when your needs are not being met, even though you know God loves you?

Week Recap

We can focus on what's eternal and trust God to provide for our necessities when we remember that our life here on Earth is temporary. Living in fear of losing our valued possessions can trap us, but having faith in Jesus gives us eternal life, spiritual abundance, and strength to face difficult trials.

For all these things do the nations of the world seek after: and your Father knoweth that ye have need of these things. But rather seek ye the kingdom of God; and all these things shall be added unto you. Fear not, little flock; for it is your Father's good pleasure to give you the kingdom.

LUKE 12:30–32 (KJV)

WEEK 30

LAVISHED WITH HIS LOVE

Reading Plan

DAY 1: Luke 13:23–35

DAY 2: Luke 14:1–14

DAY 3: Luke 14:15–24

DAY 4: Luke 14:25–35

DAY 5: Luke 15:1–10

DAY 6: Luke 15:11–32

DAY 7: Study and Reflection

Bible Study

In Luke 15's parable of the prodigal son, a young man takes his inheritance early and leaves home. When he returns in desperation after squandering it, his father—instead of being angry and turning him away—responds with great joy and lavishes him with love.

When we've distanced ourselves from God, it's easy to believe he'll no longer want anything to do with us. We may have experienced a fickle love from people, who may act hot or cold with us at different times. But the truth is, God's love does not change; it is not based on what we do or don't do.

The prodigal son exhausted all his options before returning home. Can you relate? Sometimes we hit rock bottom before we can see our own shortcomings. Or you may relate more to the older brother's feelings, and it's hard for you to understand how God values the worst of sinners just like he values you. Most of us stray at some point in our lives, but when we confess our faults with a humble and repentant heart, we are immediately forgiven. When we've walked away from God, remember that he is waiting for us with open arms to run back to him. God lavishes us with love and renews us, taking us from lost to found.

Prayer

*Dear heavenly Father, thank you for lavishing your love on me,
even when I fail to recognize my need for you. Help me, Lord,
not to rely on my own strength. In Jesus' name I pray. Amen.*

Prompts, Reflections, Actions

OBSERVE

- What did the younger son do with his inheritance in the parable of the prodigal son? How would you feel if he were your son?

- What did the father do when he saw his prodigal son coming home? Does his reaction seem fair to you?

- How did the older brother of the prodigal son respond to his younger brother's return? Was he justified in this response?

- Review Luke 15:1. Why do you think it was so important for Jesus to tell this story, considering his audience?

REFLECT

- Do you ever find it hard to believe and accept that God pours his love on you, no matter what?

- After reflecting on the story of the prodigal son, has anything changed about the way you view God's love for you?

APPLY

- What can you remember about God's love even when you're struggling and feel far from him?

- What are some ways you can respond to being lavished by God's love?

Week Recap

This week, we're reminded of God's unchanging love for us. When we encounter the pitfalls of trusting in ourselves, we can acknowledge our need for a Savior and return to God with a humble and repentant heart.

And he said unto him, Son, thou art ever with me,
and all that I have is thine. It was meet that we should
make merry, and be glad: for this thy brother was
dead, and is alive again; and was lost, and is found.

LUKE 15:31–32 (KJV)

WEEK 31

FAITHFUL STEWARDSHIP

Reading Plan

DAY 1: Luke 16:1–15

DAY 2: Luke 16:16–31

DAY 3: Luke 17:1–10

DAY 4: Luke 17:11–19

DAY 5: Luke 17:20–30

DAY 6: Luke 17:31–37

DAY 7: Study and Reflection

Bible Study

In this week's readings, we continue to hear Jesus' teachings and parables and learn that God abundantly meets our spiritual needs so that we can, in turn, do good and bless others. We are called to mindfully look after the resources God has given us and to use what we have to serve his kingdom. This entails being wise with our earthly treasures and using the time, freedom, abilities, and talents God has entrusted to us to serve others.

We may be tempted to compare ourselves with others who seem to have more than we do as God gives different gifts to different people. But what matters is that we make the most of what we do have. There may be seasons when we have a lot and others when we have less. When we make the most of what we have been given, we acknowledge the fact that everything God has given us really belongs to him. When we do this, he can then entrust us with more abundance, because he knows that what he's given us will be used to serve his kingdom.

When we are faithful with all we've been given, we can know we are fulfilling our highest calling of all: to glorify God. And when we do God's will even in the tasks that feel mundane to us in the day-to-day, we may find that he eventually trusts us to do greater things that we couldn't even imagine for his kingdom!

Prayer

Dear heavenly Father, please help me to be a wise and faithful steward of everything you have entrusted to me. May I use my special gifts to serve your kingdom and glorify your name. In Jesus' name I pray. Amen.

Prompts, Reflections, Actions

OBSERVE

- What did Jesus say about those who are faithful in little ways in Luke 16:10?

- What did Jesus say about serving God and money in Luke 16:13?

- In the parable of Lazarus and the rich man, what happened to each character after they died?

REFLECT

- How can you keep a healthy perspective around worldly goods?

- Everything we have belongs to God. How does knowing this affect your relationship with your possessions and resources?

- What does it mean to you to be a faithful steward?

APPLY

- At times when you don't have much to give, you can trust that
  God can do a lot with even a little. How can you care for and show
  gratitude for what you have?

- What are some practical ways you can use your time, talent, and
  treasures to serve God's kingdom and bless others?

- What are some ways you can be vigilant to keep money or possessions
  from becoming idols?

Week Recap

God has given us everything we have, including our time, talent, and
treasures. He calls us to be faithful stewards and use these resources wisely to
glorify God and bless others. When we do so, we fulfill our highest calling.

He that is faithful in that which is least is faithful also in much:
and he that is unjust in the least is unjust also in much.

LUKE 16:10 (KJV)

What Is Good Enough?

Reading Plan

DAY 1: Luke 18:1–14

DAY 2: Luke 18:15–27

DAY 3: Matthew 19:1–12

DAY 4: Matthew 19:13–30

DAY 5: Mark 10:1–12

DAY 6: Mark 10:13–27

DAY 7: Study and Reflection

Bible Study

In this week's readings, Jesus tells the story of a Pharisee and a tax collector. The Pharisee flaunts his religiousness to publicly display his devotion to God, while the tax collector, knowing that he is a sinner, stands at a distance, feeling unworthy of even looking up toward heaven. Outwardly, the Pharisee is more righteous than the tax collector. But Jesus points out that the tax collector approaches God with a humble heart. He acknowledges both his sin and his need for God's mercy and forgiveness. The Pharisee, on the other hand, is too busy promoting himself to make room in his heart for God.

It's tempting to try to measure whether we're good enough by how good we appear compared with others, and it may cause us to feel insecure in our worth. But our "goodness" is not measured by anything we do. Rather, it is solely based on what Jesus has done for us. It is our honesty, transparency, and humility before God that bring us to a place where we can believe and receive God's forgiveness, which is offered to us only through our faith in Jesus.

Prayer

Dear heavenly Father, please forgive me for the times
when I allow pride and self-righteousness to creep in. Help
me receive your love with gratitude and humility, not as
something that is earned. In Jesus' name I pray. Amen.

Prompts, Reflections, Actions

OBSERVE

- What was the Pharisee's attitude toward the tax collector?

- How did the tax collector approach God?

- How did the Pharisee and the tax collector differ in response to their own sin?

REFLECT

- We are free to approach God because of Jesus, even in all our imperfections. How do you respond to this generous grace?

- The tax collector acknowledged his sin and pled for God's mercy and forgiveness. What can be learned from this?

APPLY

- How can you avoid falling into the trap of comparing yourself with others to measure your own virtuousness?

- How can you encourage yourself and your loved ones to come before God, to remember that we can receive salvation simply by having faith in Jesus?

Week Recap

Our "goodness" is based not on what we do but solely on what Jesus has done for us. We don't need to measure our worth against others but should instead approach God with honesty, transparency, and humility and receive his forgiveness, love, and mercy through faith in Jesus.

And they that heard it said, Who then can
be saved? And he said, The things which are
impossible with men are possible with God.

LUKE 18:26–27 (KJV)

The Upside-Down Kingdom

Reading Plan

DAY 1: Matthew 20:1–16

DAY 2: Matthew 20:17–28

DAY 3: Matthew 20:29–34

DAY 4: Mark 10:28–45

DAY 5: Mark 10:46–52

DAY 6: Luke 18:28–43

DAY 7: Study and Reflection

Bible Study

As believers, it's discouraging when we try our best, do the work, check all the boxes, but see others, some even newer in faith, experiencing God's blessings—blessings we had wanted for ourselves. Instead, we are disappointed by unmet expectations.

There's nothing wrong with asking God for what we desire. He wants to hear from us. But it's all too easy to fall into the trap of believing we are entitled to certain things or demanding our prayers be answered the way we want them to be. We may believe we are more deserving of God's blessing than someone else because of the things we've accomplished or how virtuous or upright we have been. Our pride can cause us to seek glory for ourselves rather than serve God.

However, the kingdom of God is known as an upside-down kingdom because while the world measures status by wealth, position, and power—by accomplishments and accolades—in God's eyes, those who are willing to be last are considered to be great. Sometimes choosing to be last can feel like we are less worthy than others and even invisible. But remember: Jesus *chose* to be last by living the life of a servant. Like him, we are also called to lay down our lives and put others ahead of ourselves. Our reward is the unfathomable gift of God's grace, which is more than we could ever earn or deserve.

Prayer

Dear heavenly Father, please help me to be humble so
that I can serve you wholeheartedly, without seeking glory
or comparing my blessings with others'. I trust in your
goodness and grace alone. In Jesus' name I pray. Amen.

Prompts, Reflections, Actions

OBSERVE

- In the parable of the workers in the vineyard in Matthew 20, how did the landowner justify paying all the workers the same wage?

- How did the first hired workers react when they found out that the workers who were hired later were paid the same wages?

- In Matthew 20:24–28, when the other disciples heard about what Jesus granted James and John, how did they react?

REFLECT

- Many of us struggle with comparing ourselves with others in terms of accomplishments or blessings. How can you work toward overcoming that?

- Recall a time when serving others brought you joy and fulfillment in your life.

APPLY

- How do you combat feelings of entitlement and cultivate a heart of gratitude?

- In what ways can you intentionally serve others this week, without expecting anything in return?

Week Recap

As humans, we are prone to feeling entitled and seeking glory for ourselves. Instead, we can willingly serve God and others, even if it means being willing to be last. The kingdom of God values humility and service, and God rewards us with his grace and goodness.

But many that are first shall be last; and the last first.

MARK 10:31 (KJV)

The Power of Delayed Miracles

Reading Plan

DAY 1: Luke 19:1–10

DAY 2: Luke 19:11–28

DAY 3: John 11:1–11

DAY 4: John 11:12–27

DAY 5: John 11:28–37

DAY 6: John 11:38–57

DAY 7: Study and Reflection

Bible Study

Have you ever felt like it's too late to get help? Or have you ever prayed about something but doubted God's timing in answering? In this week's readings, sisters Mary and Martha send urgent word to Jesus. Their brother Lazarus is gravely ill, and they ask Jesus to come and help him. Jesus doesn't rush to their aid, though; in fact, when he does finally arrive at their house, Lazarus is already dead and in the tomb. Martha and Mary both exclaim that if only Jesus had arrived sooner, he could have healed their brother, preventing his death. Now, it's too late.

But Jesus goes to the tomb and raises Lazarus from the dead, displaying his power as the Son of God. This miracle would not have been possible if

Jesus had simply healed Lazarus earlier. Because of his delayed timing, many witnessed the glory of God and came to believe in Jesus.

When God delays a specific promise, we might worry that he has forgotten about us—just as Martha and Mary must've felt as they waited at their brother's bedside. But his delay does not indicate a lesser love. Jesus' response in weeping for Lazarus showed that he was also touched by grief. He understands how we feel and may even feel what we go through right along with us.

Jesus came through for his friends just as he comes through for us. Sometimes the wait for God to relieve us of our pain can feel unbearable. But trusting in his intentional timing can help us see that he may have an even bigger miracle in store for us.

Prayer

Dear heavenly Father, help me to trust in your timing and
have faith that you always work for our good, even in times
of delay and uncertainty. In Jesus' name I pray. Amen.

Prompts, Reflections, Actions

OBSERVE

- How did Jesus respond when he received news of Lazarus' sickness?

- How long had Lazarus been dead by the time Jesus arrived?

- What did Jesus say before he raised Lazarus from the dead?

REFLECT

- Have you ever experienced a delayed promise from God? How did it feel and what was the outcome?

- Are there any areas in your life where you feel like God is delaying on giving you an answer to a prayer?

APPLY

- How can you grow in your faith, even through times of delay or uncertainty?

- Times of waiting are hard for everyone. Name some things that you find or found to be encouraging in seasons of waiting.

Week Recap

In John 11, Jesus receives news of his dear friend Lazarus' sickness and yet does not rush to his aid. Upon arrival, Jesus raises Lazarus from the dead, demonstrating his power and compassion. Delayed promises from God don't mean he loves us any less. He may be preparing an even bigger miracle.

Jesus saith unto her, Said I not unto thee, that, if thou wouldest believe, thou shouldest see the glory of God? Then they took away the stone from the place where the dead was laid. And Jesus lifted up his eyes, and said, Father, I thank thee that thou hast heard me.

JOHN 11:40-41 (KJV)

An Unexpected King

Reading Plan

DAY 1: Luke 19:28–40

DAY 2: Luke 19:41–48

DAY 3: Matthew 21:1–16

DAY 4: Mark 11:1–18

DAY 5: John 12:1–11

DAY 6: John 12:12–19

DAY 7: Study and Reflection

Bible Study

In this week's passages, we see Jesus leave Bethphage from the Mount of Olives and ride triumphantly into Jerusalem on a donkey. The multitudes wave palm branches as they celebrate Jesus, proclaiming him to be their long-expected Messiah. But a few days later, a crowd—containing many of the very same people—abandons Jesus to be crucified. Perhaps this is because he failed to fulfill the onlookers' expectations or because they were expecting a king on a throne rather than a servant king. They did not understand God's plan.

That fickle crowd is a reminder of how we can often have a limited understanding of the intricacies of God's plan. Sometimes we want Jesus to meet our agenda and expectations, and when we don't get our way, it can be easy to turn our backs on God. But times like those are when faith can step in and help us to realize that Jesus is *exactly* the Messiah we need. It might mean understanding that God allows friction in our lives if it allows a higher purpose to be accomplished for our good. When we reflect on how Jesus conquered sin through his sacrifice on the cross, we can triumph knowing that even when we don't appear to be winning the battle, we can claim the victory that Jesus has already won.

Prayer

Dear heavenly Father, help me to recognize your ultimate plan and not be swayed by my worldly desires. I pray for your guidance as I seek a deeper relationship with you. In Jesus' name I pray. Amen.

Prompts, Reflections, Actions

OBSERVE

- What objects did the crowd wave to celebrate Jesus' triumphant entry into Jerusalem, and what do they signify?

- What did the people shout as Jesus entered Jerusalem?

- What was the Old Testament prophecy that foretold this event? Why did the authors of the Gospels choose to point it out?

REFLECT

• In what ways have you been fickle in your faith?

• How can you focus on your spiritual growth so that you can remain grounded when things don't go your way?

• Can you recall a time when you allowed God to lead you even though you weren't sure of the outcome? Was it challenging to let him lead? How did things turn out?

APPLY

- Where in your life can you trust more deeply in God's plan for you?

- One way to strengthen your faith is to be in constant conversation with God. If you don't have a regular practice of prayer, try to stay in dialogue as you go about your day this week. What other steps can you take to grow spiritually?

Week Recap

The triumphant entry of Jesus into Jerusalem on a donkey was initially celebrated by the crowds with palm branches and shouts of "Hosanna!" However, their expectations for a political savior were not met, leading many to abandon Jesus. Similarly, when our own faith is fickle and based on our expectations rather than trusting in God's will, it can cause us to abandon our relationship with him.

And the multitudes that went before, and that followed,
cried, saying, Hosanna to the son of David: Blessed is
he that cometh in the name of the Lord; Hosanna in the
highest. And when he was come into Jerusalem, all the
city was moved, saying, Who is this? And the multitude
said, This is Jesus the prophet of Nazareth of Galilee.

MATTHEW 21:9–11 (KJV)

FRUITFUL
FAITH

Reading Plan

DAY 1: Matthew 21:17-27

DAY 2: Matthew 21:28-46

DAY 3: Mark 11:19-33

DAY 4: Mark 12:1-12

DAY 5: Luke 20:1-8

DAY 6: Luke 20:9-18

DAY 7: Study and Reflection

Bible Study

When we begin to see our life as a walk with Jesus, it changes us. Our actions begin to reflect the fruits of the Spirit: love, joy, peace, patience, kindness, goodness, faithfulness, gentleness, and self-control (Galatians 5:22–23). These qualities are not something we need to force by our own efforts but a natural outcome of cultivating our relationship with Jesus.

In this week's passages, we see Jesus speaking on the importance of bearing spiritual fruit. A fruitful faith grows out of a consistent prayer life and time in the Word, because when we spend time with Jesus, we learn to be more and more like him. For example, experiencing forgiveness from God enables us to be more willing to share that same forgiveness to others. When we've experienced hurt from others and it feels impossible to forgive, God can help us get free from any resentment or bitterness we may be experiencing. When we are challenged to forgive those who've hurt us, we can remember that God pursues us in all circumstances. Remembering that he forgives and loves us even when we're undeserving of his forgiveness can help us to courageously extend the same blessing to others and receive it for ourselves.

Prayer

Dear heavenly Father, help me to bear the fruit of the Spirit in my life and to forgive as you have forgiven me. Help me to abide in you and grow in my faith. In Jesus' name I pray. Amen.

Prompts, Reflections, Actions

OBSERVE

- In Mark 11, who did Jesus can say can move mountains with their faith?

- In Matthew 21:22, what is the key component of receiving what we ask for in prayer?

- What is required of us in order to obtain forgiveness from our Father?

REFLECT

- Why is forgiveness important for spiritual growth?

- Is there anyone in your life you need to forgive? How can you extend forgiveness to them?

- Can you recall a time when you asked for or received forgiveness from someone? How did it unfold?

APPLY

- Where can you prioritize and insert more prayer in your daily routine?

- Is there someone in your life or in the Bible who exemplifies the fruit of the Spirit? What can you learn from them to help you apply those qualities to your own life?

Week Recap

Jesus emphasizes the importance of bearing spiritual fruit—which in turn is a reflection of our relationship with him. Consistent prayer and intentional time in God's Word are key elements of a fruitful faith.

Jesus answered and said unto them, Verily I say unto you, If ye have faith, and doubt not, ye shall not only do this which is done to the fig tree, but also if ye shall say unto this mountain, Be thou removed, and be thou cast into the sea; it shall be done.

MATTHEW 21:21 (KJV)

GOD OF THE LIVING

Reading Plan

DAY 1: Matthew 22:1–14

DAY 2: Matthew 22:15–22

DAY 3: Matthew 22:23–33

DAY 4: Mark 12:13–27

DAY 5: Luke 20:20–26

DAY 6: Luke 20:27–40

DAY 7: Study and Reflection

Bible Study

In this week's readings, we see Jesus' enemies attempting to entrap him by asking him unanswerable questions. They're hoping he will say something that would justify his arrest. One of the questions they ask is about a hypothetical scenario in which a woman's husband passes away, so the husband's brother takes her as his wife. When *that* husband passes away, the next brother marries her—and so on, until she has been married to each of the seven brothers, all of whom die. (It was custom for brothers to do this if the woman had no sons, as a way of offering protection to the widow.) The interrogators, the Sadducees, who don't believe in resurrection after death, ask Jesus whose wife the woman would be in the afterlife.

They are perplexed when Jesus says there is no marriage in heaven—that we will be like the angels there, with boundless love and eternal relationships.

The Sadducees viewed their future through the lens of their current material world. And even though we, as believers, live in hope and faith of the next life, it's easy to imagine that our eternal reality will be comparable to our earthly reality. We may be focused on what we can physically see here, like the endless cleaning that needs to be done or the fact that we are beginning to experience the effects of aging and to be discouraged by it. But through the resurrection of Jesus, we can have hope in the promise of eternal life and the hope of a future that far surpasses our earthly existence.

Prayer

Dear heavenly Father, help me to have a deeper understanding of your truth and to see beyond my own limited perspective. I desire to fully embrace the promise of eternal life through the resurrection of Jesus Christ. In Jesus' name I pray. Amen.

Prompts, Reflections, Actions

OBSERVE

- Why were Jesus' enemies asking him questions?

- How did the Sadducees try to trap Jesus with their question about marriage in the afterlife? Why did Jesus' response surprise them?

REFLECT

- What does it mean to you to be given new life in Christ? How does that broaden your perspective?

- Why is the bodily resurrection of Jesus important to your faith?

APPLY

- What does living a new kind of life, abundant with God's love and grace, look like for you?

- How does your belief in the promise of eternal life impact your day-to-day?

Week Recap

During Passover week, Jesus' enemies attempted to entrap him with questions about the resurrection. The Sadducees, who did not believe in resurrection, asked a hypothetical question about marriage in the afterlife. Jesus responded that there is no marriage in heaven, and the Sadducees' limited thinking highlights the importance of seeking a deeper understanding of God's eternal truth.

Jesus answered and said unto them, Ye do err, not knowing the scriptures, nor the power of God. For in the resurrection they neither marry, nor are given in marriage, but are as the angels of God in heaven. But as touching the resurrection of the dead, have ye not read that which was spoken unto you by God, saying, I am the God of Abraham, and the God of Isaac, and the God of Jacob? God is not the God of the dead, but of the living.

MATTHEW 22:29–32 (KJV)

THE FOUNDATION OF SELFLESS LOVE

Reading Plan

DAY 1: Matthew 22:34–46

DAY 2: Matthew 23:1–16

DAY 3: Matthew 23:17–39

DAY 4: Mark 12:28–37

DAY 5: Mark 12:38–44

DAY 6: Luke 20:41–47

DAY 7: Study and Reflection

Bible Study

In this week's readings, Jesus boils all of the commandments down into two simple things. First, we are to love God with all our heart, soul, and mind. And second, we are to love others just as he loves them—just as he loves us.

It's amazing, isn't it? The creator of the universe is completely devoted to us and, in return, asks for our complete devotion to him. He *wants* to be in relationship with us! Not with some perfect, flawless version of us—not us only smarter, not us only more accomplished—just us, as we are, right now.

Loving God with all that we have is the foundation of our relationship with him. It means we put God first in all aspects of our lives and try to honor him in everything we do—in our relationships, in the way we talk, in the way we use our resources, gifts, and talents. God returns our love and surpasses it with his own. From this abundance, we are able to love and serve others with that same selfless love that Christ showed us. It is because God fills us up with his love for us that we have a replenished supply to give away. We run into problems when we put our love for people, ourselves, or anything else before God and develop an unhealthy attachment when we attempt to meet needs that only God is meant to fulfill.

Our love for God should motivate us to love others, and our love for others should reflect our love for God. When we follow these two inseparable commandments, everything else falls into place.

Prayer

Dear heavenly Father, help me to love you with all my heart, soul, and mind and to love my neighbors as myself. May my love for you motivate me to love others and honor your will. In Jesus' name I pray. Amen.

Prompts, Reflections, Actions

OBSERVE

* What was the context of Jesus' teaching on the greatest commandments in Matthew 22 and Mark 12?

* What are the two greatest commandments according to Jesus?

- Which Old Testament book did Jesus quote when answering the question about the greatest commandment in Matthew 22?

REFLECT

- Time is a precious gift. Think ahead about how you'll spend your time this week. How can you plan your days to reflect where your deepest affections lie?

- How does loving others reflect your love for God?

APPLY

- How can you show love and kindness to those who may be difficult to love?

- What are some instances where you can look out for the interests of others?

Week Recap

Jesus teaches that the greatest commandments are to love God with our entire being and to love our neighbors as ourselves. These commandments are the foundation for all other laws and teachings. Loving God means seeking his will and putting him first in our lives. Loving others means serving them and sharing from the abundant love that we have been given.

Jesus said unto him, Thou shalt love the Lord thy God with
all thy heart, and with all thy soul, and with all thy mind.
This is the first and great commandment. And the second
is like unto it, Thou shalt love thy neighbour as thyself.

MATTHEW 22:37-39 (KJV)

Finding Hope in Darkness

Reading Plan

DAY 1: Matthew 24:1–14

DAY 2: Matthew 24:15–31

DAY 3: Mark 13:1–13

DAY 4: Mark 13:14–27

DAY 5: Luke 21:1–19

DAY 6: Luke 21:20–27

DAY 7: Study and Reflection

Bible Study

When we read Jesus' words about the signs that the end times are nearing and about his second coming, it can feel overwhelming. The chaos and brokenness in our world today and our fears about the future is a heavy burden to carry and navigate through.

This is a good time to shift our perspective. It's in these frightening moments we must remember that we are never alone, even in the midst of troubles, even if watching the news makes us feel like the world is crumbling around us. When we keep our eyes on Jesus, there is nothing to fear. The Bible gives us a clear vision of what's happening, and we can be comforted knowing this is all part of God's bigger plan.

Fortunately, God always looks out for his children and protects us despite the tragedy in the world. In uncertain times, we don't need to ignore what happens around us, but we can live with an eternal perspective. We can have peace knowing for certain where we will be in eternity. Today's calamities can prompt us to share the good news of Jesus to others. The darker the world is, the brighter the light is, meaning we have an even greater opportunity to be a light in the darkness. In an ever-changing world, we can cling to the promises of a never-changing God.

Prayer

Dear heavenly Father, help me to have faith and trust in your plan as I navigate through the darkness in this world. Help me to be bold and share your hope with those around me. In Jesus' name I pray. Amen.

Prompts, Reflections, Actions

OBSERVE

- What are some of the specific signs of the end times mentioned in Matthew 24 and Mark 13?

- What did Jesus say about false messiahs and false prophets in these chapters?

- In Mark 13:7, what did Jesus instruct about how to respond to hearing of wars?

REFLECT

- What does it mean to have an eternal perspective in uncertain times?

- When you're feeling overwhelmed and frightened by uncertain times, what do your prayers look like?

APPLY

- What gives you hope in the midst of chaos and brokenness in this world? Identify what you are hopeful for today.

- In what ways can you share the hope of the Gospel with those around you and be a light in the darkness?

Week Recap

Jesus speaks about the things that will signal his second coming. These signs are overwhelming and frightening, but they also indicate Christ's wonderful return. As Christians, we can find hope and solace in Jesus' words and the opportunity to be a light in the darkness.

And then shall appear the sign of the Son of man
in heaven: and then shall all the tribes of the earth
mourn, and they shall see the Son of man coming in
the clouds of heaven with power and great glory.

MATTHEW 24:30 (KJV)

Preparing for Jesus' Coming

Reading Plan

DAY 1: Matthew 24:32–41

DAY 2: Matthew 24:42–51

DAY 3: Matthew 25:1–13

DAY 4: Matthew 25:14–30

DAY 5: Mark 13:28–37

DAY 6: Luke 21:28–38

DAY 7: Study and Reflection

Bible Study

As believers, we eagerly await Jesus' return. Although we do not know the day or the hour he'll come, he tells us in Matthew 24 to be watchful and ready for his arrival. Our lives change dramatically when we live with the expectation that Jesus could return at any moment. One of my greatest desires that gives me purpose every day is to hear Jesus say, "Well done, my good and faithful servant," when I finally run into his arms.

Becoming a good and faithful servant can look like using our talents and resources to serve God and others and by finding ways to share the Gospel message with those around us. It looks like prioritizing our relationships so that we can share his love with others. I regret many seasons in my life when I focused more on pursuing my own kingdom rather than serving God's kingdom. For me, being a good and faithful servant means moving away from trying to create a perfect, put-together life for myself and moving closer to prioritizing my relationships above my ambitions, because I now see my time with people as valuable opportunities to serve those who are precious to God.

Prioritizing his kingdom can take many forms: We can be in community with one another to serve God and uplift each other. We can cultivate our own ability to discern God's will and then make our choices in life accordingly. We can set aside sacred time within each day to pray and study the Bible, and we can surround ourselves with wise people who can offer guidance along the journey. We can accept all the love and forgiveness and blessing that God offers and then share it with those who cross our path. It can be simply smiling at a stranger in the grocery store or listening and offering comfort when a friend needs support.

When we honor God today by being faithful wherever he has currently planted us, we don't need to worry about when, exactly, Jesus will arrive.

Prayer

Dear heavenly Father, help me to be ready and watchful for your return. May I live as a faithful servant, using my talents and resources to serve you and share the Gospel message with others as your daughter. In Jesus' name I pray. Amen.

Prompts, Reflections, Actions

OBSERVE

- In Matthew 24, what did Jesus say about the timing of his return?

- In Matthew 25, Jesus used a parable to teach a lesson about being prepared for his coming. In the story, how did the five wise virgins prepare, and what was the outcome?

- According to Luke 21, what should we do as we wait for the return of Jesus Christ?

REFLECT

- How does knowing that Jesus could return at any moment impact how you live your life?

- What are some of God's promises that comfort you?

APPLY

- If you knew that Jesus was returning this very day, how would you use your talents and resources right now?

- What are some daily or weekly actions you can take to cultivate a heart of readiness for Christ's return?

Week Recap

We eagerly await the promised return of Jesus Christ, and although we don't know the exact time, we live our lives in anticipation of his coming. We are called to be good and faithful servants, using the gifts we've been given to serve God and others and to share the Gospel message.

His lord said unto him, Well done, thou good and faithful
servant: thou hast been faithful over a few things, I will make
thee ruler over many things: enter thou into the joy of thy lord.

MATTHEW 25:21 (KJV)

WHOLEHEARTED DEVOTION

Reading Plan

DAY 1: Matthew 25:31–46

DAY 2: Matthew 26:1–13

DAY 3: Mark 14:1–11

DAY 4: Luke 22:1–13

DAY 5: John 12:20–36

DAY 6: John 12:37–50

DAY 7: Study and Reflection

Bible Study

In the last week before his crucifixion, Mary expresses her complete devotion to Jesus by blessing him with an alabaster jar of precious oil. While the disciples grumble that the expensive oil is a waste of money that could have been given to the poor instead, Jesus praises Mary for expressing her devotion.

Our busy lives are filled with work, relationships, responsibilities, and tasks that occupy our attention. Sometimes at the end of the day, we may feel like we don't have much to offer to God. Wouldn't it be better to take Mary's attitude and give Jesus the best of what we have rather than only what's left when everything else is gone? Prioritizing our relationship with God means being willing to give him what's most precious to us—bringing our devotion to him into every facet of our lives.

Where in our lives can we more fully dedicate ourselves to God? When we remember who we are and *whose* we are, we can be bold in our faith, realizing that there are countless ways to express our devotion, in everything from how we treat the people in our lives to how we look after God's creation. When we are fully devoted to him, we no longer worry about what it may cost us.

Prayer

Dear heavenly Father, I want to remain wholeheartedly devoted to you like Mary, giving you my best even when it costs me. I pray for a bold and courageous faith. In Jesus' name I pray. Amen.

Prompts, Reflections, Actions

OBSERVE

- How did Jesus respond to the disciples when they saw Mary anointing him with precious oil?

- In John 12:23–24, what did Jesus say must occur for him to be glorified?

- In John 12:49–50, whom did Jesus name as the source of his words?

REFLECT

- List some things that are difficult for you to give up for God (e.g., time, money, negative habits).

APPLY

- What are some practical ways you can give God your all in your daily life?

- What are some things you value and cherish? How can you dedicate them to God?

- What are some things that might discourage your relationship with God? What fuels your faith, and how do you continually nourish and deepen it?

Week Recap

Mary demonstrated her complete love and devotion to Jesus through a beautiful gesture of anointing him with expensive oil. When we, like Mary, give our best to Jesus, we can experience the pure joy and fulfillment that come from wholeheartedly devoting ourselves to him.

For in that she hath poured this ointment on my body, she did it for my burial. Verily I say unto you, Wheresoever this gospel shall be preached in the whole world, there shall also this, that this woman hath done, be told for a memorial of her.

MATTHEW 26:12–13 (KJV)

Becoming a Servant Leader

Reading Plan

DAY 1: Matthew 26:14-25

DAY 2: Mark 14:12-26

DAY 3: Luke 22:14-30

DAY 4: John 13: 1-11

DAY 5: John 13:12-20

DAY 6: John 13:21-30

DAY 7: Study and Reflection

Bible Study

Jesus was full of surprises. As his departure from the world was nearing, he knelt before his disciples and washed their feet. Like our world today, being served by others was an ultimate display of status. Instead, Jesus chose to demonstrate the ultimate humility. The disciples must've been in shock as he lovingly washed the dust and dirt away from their feet. Here was God himself, having taken on human form, faithfully serving them—treating with love even the one who would betray him. It must've been hard to accept such a blessing. They must have felt unworthy.

It's *still* hard to fathom that our King would take the time to help us in our weak and soiled state. But the example of Jesus insisting on serving his disciples can remind us of how he washes away our sins even though we are unworthy. Most of us rely on our own strength, striving to be "good enough." But the truth is, no matter how many gold stars we rack up, we could never deserve the blessing of God's forgiveness and love. But God asks us to put our hesitancy aside and humble ourselves to receive his grace by bringing our weaknesses, sins, and mistakes to him and to let him wash them away. Newly clean and whole, we can return the blessing by sharing it with others.

Prayer

Dear heavenly Father, help me to follow the example of Jesus by humbly serving others. I bring to you all my sin and weaknesses for cleansing. Thank you! In Jesus' name I pray. Amen.

Prompts, Reflections, Actions

OBSERVE

- How did the disciples initially react to Jesus washing their feet?

- What did Jesus tell Judas after he gave him a piece of bread?

- What led Peter to change his mind about having his feet washed by Jesus?

REFLECT

- What can you say to God when you bring your brokenness and weakness to him for forgiveness and cleansing? If God already knows your sins, why do you think he desires for you to boldly reveal these things to him?

- Why do you think it isn't always easy for us to bring our weaknesses to God?

APPLY

- How can you actively work to serve others with the kind of love Jesus showed in serving his disciples?

- Where is Jesus leading you with your gifts to follow his example?

Week Recap

As Jesus' departure from the world was nearing, he humbly washed his disciples' feet. This act was not just an example of service but a symbol of how Jesus washes us of our sin.

Ye call me Master and Lord: and ye say well; for so I am. If I then, your Lord and Master, have washed your feet; ye also ought to wash one another's feet.

JOHN 13:13–14 (KJV)

KNOWN BY LOVE

Reading Plan

DAY 1: Matthew 26:26–35

DAY 2: Mark 14:27–31

DAY 3: Luke 22:31–39

DAY 4: John 13:31–38

DAY 5: John 14:1–14

DAY 6: John 14:15–31

DAY 7: Study and Reflection

Bible Study

What, exactly, is love? Often, we frame it as what makes us happy, what someone does for us, how they make us feel, how we express it to others, or how we feel toward them. But the Bible presents a much more complete picture of love.

In John 14:21, Jesus explains that obeying his commandments is the ultimate way to demonstrate our love for him. That means that love motivates our obedience to him. In other words, our obedience to God is not about doing everything perfectly and performing on our own strength but about outwardly expressing our love for Jesus.

It is important for us as believers to embody God's love, as Jesus said that others will recognize us as his followers by our love. Apart from God, it's difficult to love purely and unconditionally without any hidden motives. When we're deeply rooted in God's love, however, he empowers us to love the way Jesus did. Love becomes the key ingredient in everything we do—it is the root of our actions and choices. It is self-sacrificial (1 Corinthians 13). When we love someone, it compels us to act in their best interest from a pure heart.

Prayer

Dear heavenly Father, thank you for the greatest love I have ever received. Help me to love others in a way that will draw them closer to you. In Jesus' name I pray. Amen.

Prompts, Reflections, Actions

OBSERVE

- In John 14:6, who did Jesus say is the way, the truth, and the life? What does this mean?

- In John 14:12, what did Jesus say those who believe in him will do?

- In John 14:26, whom did Jesus say the Father would send?

REFLECT

- In what ways have you experienced the difference between the world's definition of love and the biblical definition of love?

- Are there any areas of your life where something else is captivating your heart more than Jesus?

- How has your understanding of God's love for you affected how you love others?

- What are some steps you can take to focus your heart on Jesus this week?

- What are some practical ways you can demonstrate love to others?

Week Recap

According to the world, "love" is often based on feelings. However, the Bible defines love as self-sacrificial. When we love others, it compels us to act in their best interest, and our obedience to Jesus' commandments is an outflow of our love for him.

A new commandment I give unto you, That ye love one another; as I have loved you, that ye also love one another. By this shall all men know that ye are my disciples, if ye have love one to another.

JOHN 13:34–35 (KJV)

COMPLETE JOY

Reading Plan

DAY 1: John 15:1-17

DAY 2: John 15:18-27

DAY 3: John 16:1-16

DAY 4: John 16:17-33

DAY 5: John 17:1-19

DAY 6: John 17:20-26

DAY 7: Study and Reflection

Bible Study

Waiting is hard. Whether we're waiting for the next milestone in our lives, waiting for the answer to a question, waiting for a new chapter to begin—it's challenging, and the anxiety is real. But there is a joy and peace that comes from God that frees us from the anxiousness that we often experience while we wait. The Bible tells us we can have joy even in the midst of difficult circumstances because they help us grow and mature spiritually (James 1:2–4). This doesn't mean everything will come easy to us—Christians endure struggles just like everyone else. But the difference comes in knowing that in God's presence, we can experience complete joy that transcends our earthly circumstances (Psalm 16:11).

In this week's readings, Jesus reassures his disciples that after his death, the Holy Spirit will be their comforter and guide them with the spirit of truth. The same is true for us. When we abide in God, we can receive a joy and peace that exceeds any that the world can offer. In God, our hopes have no limit, and we can rest in the comfort of knowing that he can provide eternal peace for his children, even as we wait.

Prayer

Dear heavenly Father, thank you for the joy that I find in your presence. Help me to focus on your truth when I feel worried and restless. In Jesus' name I pray. Amen.

Prompts, Reflections, Actions

OBSERVE

- In John 15, what analogy did Jesus use to describe his relationship with his disciples?

- In John 16, what did Jesus tell his disciples about the coming of the Holy Spirit?

- In John 17, what did Jesus pray for his disciples?

REFLECT

- Have you ever found yourself waiting for the next milestone in your life? Did it arrive? What were you challenged by in the waiting?

- In times of waiting, what might comfort you and remind you that God can offer you everlasting joy and peace?

APPLY

- What can you do today to seek joy and peace?

- How can you extend joy and peace to others?

Week Recap

God's joy and peace surpasses the happiness found from the pursuit of worldly achievements. To bear the fruit of the Spirit, including joy and peace, we must abide in God. This joy and peace are based on everlasting truths and can be experienced even in difficult circumstances.

If ye abide in me, and my words abide in you, ye shall ask what ye will, and it shall be done unto you.

JOHN 15:7 (KJV)

These things have I spoken unto you, that my joy might remain in you, and that your joy might be full.

JOHN 15:11 (KJV)

SURRENDER IN SUFFERING

Reading Plan

DAY 1: Matthew 26:36-46

DAY 2: Matthew 26: 47-56

DAY 3: Mark 14:32-42

DAY 4: Mark 14:43-52

DAY 5: Luke 22:40-53

DAY 6: John 18:1-11

DAY 7: Study and Reflection

Bible Study

On the night before Jesus' death, we see him in agony over what lies ahead. He retreats to pray in the Garden of Gethsemane. *Gethsemane* means "oil press." The process of making olive oil involved using a heavy stone to crush olives to squeeze the oil from the pulp—a fitting image since Jesus was about to have the sins of the world pressed down on him. He prays fervently, admitting that he would rather somehow have this cup pass from him; he would rather not have to face the torture of the cross. But even so, in an incredible act of courage and obedience, he surrenders his will to that of his Father.

When we are struggling with challenging circumstances, our sight can get clouded. We want to take control, so surrendering to God's plan can seem like an impossible mission. We question why we are enduring pain and want to be relieved of the burdens and anguish we carry. It helps to remember that challenges like these are not wasted. Like trees with dead branches that need to be pruned to make room for fresh growth, we can be pruned when we surrender our circumstances to God, knowing that he understands and will never leave our side. Old habits and unhealthy ways of thinking are cut off to make room for new thoughts, desires, and ways aligned with a renewed life in Christ. A new path is created for us, and we are more equipped to bless others. When we can release our tight grip on what we want and open our minds to God's plan, we allow him to transform us for his glory.

Prayer

Dear heavenly Father, help me to surrender to your will in times
of suffering and trust that you can use it all for good. Prune me
and grow me for your glory. In Jesus' name I pray. Amen.

Prompts, Reflections, Actions

OBSERVE

- What did Jesus pray about at Gethsemane?

- What did the disciples do after Jesus asked them to watch and pray?

- How many times did Jesus pray to God asking him to be spared from the suffering he was about to endure on the cross? How did Jesus follow up each appeal?

REFLECT

- Have you ever been able to use your struggles to bless or sympathize with others? In what ways have you been able to learn or receive blessings through others' sharing of their challenges with you?

- How have you experienced God's pruning through pain in your life, and what new growth and maturing came from it?

APPLY

- What are some ways you can use your own painful experiences to encourage and bless others?

- How can you actively seek God's pruning in your life?

Week Recap

The night before his death, Jesus retreated to pray in the garden of Gethsemane, where he surrendered to God's will despite the suffering he knew was ahead. We can learn from his example to trust God in our own struggles, knowing that he can use our pain to bless us and others.

And he was withdrawn from them about a stone's
cast, and kneeled down, and prayed, Saying, Father, if
thou be willing, remove this cup from me: nevertheless
not my will, but thine, be done. And there appeared an
angel unto him from heaven, strengthening him.

LUKE 22:41-43 (KJV)

MISPLACED FAITH

Reading Plan

DAY 1: Matthew 26:57–68

DAY 2: Matthew 26:69–75

DAY 3: Mark 14:53–65

DAY 4: Mark 14:66–72

DAY 5: Luke 22:54–71

DAY 6: John 18:12–27

DAY 7: Study and Reflection

Bible Study

There was a time when I thought I was at the height of my faith. I believed nothing could shatter my faith, like a spiritual high. But I was in for a shock when I encountered a challenge and I realized that it was so easy to doubt that God would come through for me. It turned out my faith was in *my own belief* rather than in God.

It's a common pitfall to make the object of our faith something other than God. This week we see Peter, so confident in himself, saying that he could never deny Jesus. But when Peter realizes that he has failed in this, he is broken and weeps bitterly.

Just like Peter, we often allow pride to seep in and become overconfident in our own strength. This is exactly the moment we become susceptible to falling. Peter was humbled by his own shortcomings and was able to acknowledge them, and he was instantly forgiven. Likewise, when we come to God in repentance for our failures, he shows us his unending mercy and forgiveness—and this, in turn, deepens our faith. We all fall short. That's part of being human. God invites us to come as we are, but he doesn't force us. He may sometimes allow us to experience a fall so that we can learn to place our faith in his unwavering love, grace, and power.

Prayer

Dear heavenly Father, thank you for never failing me
even when I fail you. Grow my faith in you rather than
in my own strength. In Jesus' name I pray. Amen.

Prompts, Reflections, Actions

OBSERVE

- In Mark 14:55, what were the chief priests and the whole Sanhedrin looking to arrest Jesus for?

- What did the high priest ask Jesus during his trial? How did Jesus respond?

- Whom did Peter deny knowing three times?

REFLECT

- Think of a time when you placed confidence in your own strength. What did you learn from this?

- How does God respond when you come to him in humble repentance for your failures?

- In what areas of your life can you rely more on God's strength rather than your own?

- When you struggle with depending on God for strength, set aside a moment each day to simply ask him for help.

- When God equips your heart and mind, what does encountering failures and shortcomings in the future look like?

Week Recap

Placing confidence in our own strength can lead us to fall when challenges arise. Like Peter, we may fail, but when we come to God in repentance, he shows us his unending mercy and forgiveness. Learning to trust in God's strength and not our own makes us less susceptible to falling.

And the Lord turned, and looked upon Peter. And Peter remembered the word of the Lord, how he had said unto him, Before the cock crow, thou shalt deny me thrice. And Peter went out, and wept bitterly.

LUKE 22:61–62 (KJV)

Forgiven, Loved, and Freed

Reading Plan

DAY 1: Matthew 27:1–10

DAY 2: Matthew 27:11–26

DAY 3: Mark 15:1–15

DAY 4: Luke 23:1–5

DAY 5: Luke 23:6–12

DAY 6: Luke 23:13–25

DAY 7: Study and Reflection

Bible Study

When we are guilty of something, we may be tempted to try to ease our conscience by making excuses or blaming others. Sometimes we may even punish ourselves as Judas did and be consumed with beating ourselves up for our sins. However, when we go to God in repentance, he is quick to forgive us. Rather than staying stuck in condemnation, shame, or blame, we can go to God, knowing that he has the power to free us from our brokenness. He loves us in spite of our flawed nature.

The next time you fall into self-condemnation, remember that we can boldly come to our loving Father and admit our wrongdoing to be restored. There is no condemnation for those who are in Christ (Romans 8:1). And once restored, we can move forward into a brand-new day, forgiven, loved, and free.

Prayer

Dear heavenly Father, help me to turn away from my sins. Remind me of your unending grace and mercy and guide me to live a life pleasing to you. In Jesus' name I pray. Amen.

Prompts, Reflections, Actions

OBSERVE

• In Matthew 27:3–4, what did Judas do after he betrayed Jesus?

• What did the chief priests and elders do with the returned money in Matthew 27:6–7?

• In Mark 15:6–11, whom did the crowd want Pilate to release instead of Jesus?

REFLECT

- Judas made a terrible mistake and fell into despair. Last week, we read that Peter made the same kind of mistake—betraying Jesus—but instead, he was restored. What is the difference between the two men's responses to their sin?

- How can you remind yourself to trust in God's grace and mercy?

- Why is it sometimes so hard to accept forgiveness?

APPLY

- What can you do to avoid falling into a perpetual cycle of self-condemnation and punishing yourself for your mistakes?

- How can you face others who have been hurt by your actions?

- God grants us repentance (e.g., Acts 11:18). List some ways to remind yourself that God is always ready to free you from the burdens of your mistakes, shortcomings, and flaws.

Week Recap

When we fail, we can trust in God's grace and mercy to restore us. When we confess our sins and seek forgiveness, we can experience true freedom and live a life pleasing to God.

Then Judas, which had betrayed him, when he saw that he was condemned, repented himself, and brought again the thirty pieces of silver to the chief priests and elders, Saying, I have sinned in that I have betrayed the innocent blood. And they said, What is that to us? see thou to that. And he cast down the pieces of silver in the temple, and departed, and went and hanged himself.

MATTHEW 27:3–5 (KJV)

WEEK 48

FULLY
FORGIVEN

Reading Plan

DAY 1: Matthew 27:27–38

DAY 2: Mark 15:16–28

DAY 3: Luke 23:26–36

DAY 4: John 18:28–40

DAY 5: John 19:1–16

DAY 6: John 19:17–24

DAY 7: Study and Reflection

Bible Study

Are there people in your life who have wounded you? Maybe they've hurt you and haven't even asked to be forgiven—or perhaps they've wronged you and not fessed up to their part. Maybe they don't deserve forgiveness.

But just like Jesus, we can forgive them anyway. Not because they deserve it, not because they're worthy of it, but simply because we ourselves have been forgiven by God. When we see how Jesus was willing to forgive—even in the middle of his own painful sacrifice—surely we can find it in our hearts to set our hurt aside and extend forgiveness to others. And we might be surprised, when we do, to find that forgiving others frees *us* as well as those who have wronged us. If we are having trouble with forgiving someone, we can ask God to help us heal from the pain we endured from being wronged so that our unforgiveness does not grow into bitterness and harden our heart.

Prayer

Dear heavenly Father, thank you for forgiving me and giving me the ability to forgive others. Help me to extend grace to others and remember your perfect sacrifice. In Jesus' name I pray. Amen.

Prompts, Reflections, Actions

OBSERVE

- Who helped carry Jesus' cross?

- How did Pilate respond when the chief priests wanted Jesus to be put to death?

- Where was Jesus crucified?

REFLECT

- Can Jesus' sacrificial love shed new light on the way you think about forgiveness in your own life?

- Have you ever had trouble forgiving someone? Who is hurt the most when we refuse to forgive?

APPLY

- Is there anyone in your life you need to forgive? What steps can you take to extend forgiveness to them?

- How can you guard your heart against bitterness and resentment toward others?

- In what ways can you show forgiveness to others even when they don't deserve it?

Week Recap

Jesus' perfect sacrifice on the cross covered the debt of our sin. Because of his forgiveness that was freely given to us, we can find it within ourselves to show grace to others, forgiving those who have hurt us.

Then said Jesus, Father, forgive them; for they know not what they do. And they parted his raiment, and cast lots.

LUKE 23:34 (KJV)

IT IS FINISHED

Reading Plan

DAY 1: Matthew 27:39–50

DAY 2: Matthew 27:51–64

DAY 3: Mark 15:29–38

DAY 4: Mark 15:39–47

DAY 5: Luke 23:37–56

DAY 6: John 19:25–30

DAY 7: Study and Reflection

Bible Study

"It is finished." Those were Jesus' last words before he died. And in that moment, the debt for sinners was fully paid, and nothing could ever again separate God from his people. At the temple of Jerusalem, the veil that was used to separate God's sacred presence was torn from top to bottom, representing that from that moment on, we could all approach God through Jesus.

In our daily walk, it can be tempting to believe that we must do or achieve something to obtain God's approval and *earn* our place in heaven. We may have learned this if people in our lives have treated us differently depending on what we did for them. But when we think this way, we are placing a divider—a veil—between us and God. In this state of separation, we mistakenly think that we must work to reach God's presence.

When I place my faith in what Jesus has done, instead of what I can do, the veil is lifted, and I can rest knowing Jesus has already done everything that's needed to restore my relationship with God. God's acceptance of me has nothing to do with what I do or don't do.

Prayer

Dear heavenly Father, help me to rest in the finished work of Jesus and not try to earn the gift of salvation. Thank you for accepting me because of what he has done. In Jesus' name I pray. Amen.

Prompts, Reflections, Actions

OBSERVE

- In Matthew 27:39–50, what was written above Jesus' head?

- In Mark 15:39–47, who requested Jesus' body after he died on the cross?

- In Luke 23:43, what did Jesus tell the criminal who was crucified beside him?

REFLECT

- How does placing your faith in Jesus' work on the cross free you from a performance-based faith?

- How does knowing that Jesus has completed the work of salvation affect your relationship with God?

- How does the image of the veil tearing in the temple personally impact you?

APPLY

- In what ways can you intentionally rest in Jesus' finished work?

- How can you bring and apply some of that peace to areas of striving and struggling in your life?

Week Recap

Jesus' final words on the cross, "It is finished," signal the completion of his work of salvation. The temple veil tearing represents access to God through Jesus's death. Placing our faith in Jesus' work frees us from a performance-based faith and allows us to rest in his unconditional love, acceptance, and forgiveness.

When Jesus therefore had received the vinegar, he said, It is finished: and he bowed his head, and gave up the ghost.

JOHN 19:30 (KJV)

HE IS RISEN

Reading Plan

DAY 1: Matthew 28:1-10

DAY 2: Matthew 28:11-15

DAY 3: Mark 16:1-13

DAY 4: Luke 24:1-12

DAY 5: Luke 24:13-32

DAY 6: John 19:31-42

DAY 7: Study and Reflection

Bible Study

Following Jesus' death, the first people to encounter the empty tomb were a small group of devoted women. They went there to bless his body as was their custom, but what they found shocked them. The stone at the tomb's entrance had been rolled away, and Jesus was gone. An angel was there instead, assuring the women that they shouldn't be afraid—that Jesus had risen.

It's worthwhile to remember that women were the first to witness the empty tomb. Mary was responsible for delivering the good news of Jesus' resurrection to the disciples. Through his plan, we see God has valued and honored women— even during a period in history when they were thought to be inferior and were generally excluded. But Jesus counted them among his closest friends.

Most of us, at one time or another, feel excluded or "less than," not unlike the women who lived in Jesus' day. Isn't it wonderful to remember that Jesus came for *all* people, that no one falls outside his love, and that we, as women, have always been a valuable part of God's plan?

Prayer

Dear heavenly Father, thank you for the gift of the resurrection
and the hope it brings. Help me to live in your power
every day, and remind me that I am part of your plan and
valuable in your sight. In Jesus' name I pray. Amen.

Prompts, Reflections, Actions

OBSERVE

- Who were the first people to encounter the empty tomb after Jesus's death?

- In Matthew 28:5–7, what did the angel tell the women at the empty tomb?

- In Luke 24:9–12, how did the disciples respond to the news that Jesus had risen?

REFLECT

- Some skeptics have dismissed the resurrection account as a fabrication, but it is unlikely that the Gospel writers would have chosen women as witnesses if they wanted to concoct a story, because women were not considered credible witnesses in the culture back then. Why might God have entrusted the first sight of the empty tomb to women?

- How does reflecting on the resurrection affect the way you view your life?

- How does knowing that God values everyone impact the way you perceive those around you, especially those who are overlooked or excluded?

APPLY

- Women played a crucial role throughout Jesus' ministry and resurrection. Upon reflecting, how does that shape your perspective and identity as God's daughter?

- Knowing that God has given each one of us an important role, what can you do this week to honor your special position and carry out the good news?

Week Recap

The resurrection was a historical event that proved the authority and power of Jesus. The fact that women were witnesses to Jesus' resurrection story highlights that God has always honored women. Mary's role in delivering the good news reveals that God chooses the least expected and empowers them to carry out his plan.

And as they were afraid, and bowed down their faces to the earth, they said unto them, Why seek ye the living among the dead? He is not here, but is risen: remember how he spake unto you when he was yet in Galilee, Saying, The Son of man must be delivered into the hands of sinful men, and be crucified, and the third day rise again.

LUKE 24:5-7 (KJV)

The Great Commission

Reading Plan

DAY 1: John 20:1–10

DAY 2: John 20:11–18

DAY 3: Mark 16:14–18

DAY 4: Luke 24:33–43

DAY 5: Luke 24:44–49

DAY 6: Matthew 28:16–20

DAY 7: Study and Reflection

Bible Study

Jesus didn't leave this world without giving his disciples instructions on what to do next—and he didn't leave them alone. The book of Matthew ends with Jesus commissioning them to go far and wide, teaching and baptizing all nations, making more disciples to spread the good news of God's love. Jesus tells his friends to continue to obey his commandments and promises that he'll always be with them.

    As believers, Jesus' words are for us, too. We have received the message that we are loved and forgiven as daughters of God—but like the disciples, we, too, are called to share the good news and live by Jesus' commandments.

We encounter people who need Jesus every day. They need to hear the message that there is a solution for sin and that God desires a loving relationship with them—that he wants them to experience an abundant life full of his joy and peace. We can meet their questions with gentleness and respect, sharing the Gospel through our own testimony of how God has saved us and transformed our lives, and what he has freed us from. We can share with others how the examples of godly women in the Bible, like Ruth, Esther, and Mary, show us how to live a life that honors God so that we can walk in deep fellowship with him. Once we've witnessed the transforming power of the Gospel in our own lives, we can't help but want the whole world to know about Jesus.

Jesus empowers us and promises to be with us forever. We don't have to depend on our own abilities or powers of persuasion to impact others around us. We can trust God to work through us to draw hearts to him.

Prayer

Dear heavenly Father, help me to share the Gospel with others and trust in your power to draw hearts near to you. Thank you for the transforming power of the Gospel. In Jesus' name I pray. Amen.

Prompts, Reflections, Actions

OBSERVE

- What did Jesus instruct his disciples to do in Matthew 28?

- In Luke 24:43, what did Jesus eat to show his disciples that he was not a ghost?

- In Luke 24:44–49, what did Jesus say about the Scriptures and his death and resurrection?

REFLECT

- What are some challenges about sharing the Gospel with others?

- Describe the transformation you've experienced since receiving the Gospel.

APPLY

- Have you shared the Gospel with others?

- If someone were to ask you about your faith, how would you begin?

- Who are some people with whom you can share your own faith story?

Week Recap

In the last chapter of Matthew, Jesus instructs his disciples to share the good news of the Gospel with all nations. As believers, we're called to share the solution for sin and God's desire for a loving relationship with each of us. We can trust in God's power to draw hearts near and share the transformative power of the Gospel.

And Jesus came and spake unto them, saying, All power is given unto me in heaven and in earth. Go ye therefore, and teach all nations, baptizing them in the name of the Father, and of the Son, and of the Holy Ghost: Teaching them to observe all things whatsoever I have commanded you: and, lo, I am with you always, even unto the end of the world. Amen.

MATTHEW 28:18–20 (KJV)

LIVING IN VICTORY

Reading Plan

DAY 1: Mark 16:19–20

DAY 2: Luke 24:50–53

DAY 3: John 20:19–29

DAY 4: John 20:30–31

DAY 5: John 21:1–14

DAY 6: John 21:15–25

DAY 7: Study and Reflection

Bible Study

The Gospels end with Jesus being received into heaven and taking his place at the right hand of God. He has overcome death and forged a path for all of us, for all time, to follow into God's presence. His amazing victory belongs to all of those who put their trust in him.

But sometimes, in the clutter of our daily lives, we forget to claim that victory. Sometimes it can feel like our physical reality is more real than our spiritual reality. It's understandable. We have bills to pay, careers to pursue, relationships to maintain. We have conflicts and health challenges and a big pile of laundry that needs to be folded and put away. We lose sight of our spiritual lives and forget all about the victory that is ours to share in.

We must remember that we are called to live by faith and not by sight (2 Corinthians 5:7). When we walk by sight, we can easily allow the world to dictate our identity. While we may be a sister, daughter, mother, or spouse, our most important identity is *child of God*. Instead of losing sight of that, we can turn to God to give us what we need to walk in Jesus' victory. We can take a breath and rest, reconnect to our true identity, and allow God to work for us, through us, and with us.

Prayer

Dear heavenly Father, help me to remember my true identity in Christ as your beloved child. Help me to walk by faith, not by sight, and allow you to work through me. In Jesus' name I pray. Amen.

Prompts, Reflections, Actions

OBSERVE

- In Mark 16:19–20, where did Jesus go?

- What did the disciples do after Jesus was taken up into heaven in Luke 24:50–53?

- In John 20:19–29, how did Jesus help Thomas believe that he had really risen from the dead?

REFLECT

- In what ways have you struggled with your faith?

- What are some ways you might reconnect to your sacred identity as a child of God?

- What steps can you take to be more mindful of your spiritual reality—not just your physical reality?

- What are some truths you can meditate on this week to help you maintain a mindset of victory throughout difficult situations you may encounter?

Week Recap

As believers, we can claim the victory of Jesus, but it can be challenging to live in our spiritual reality. By focusing on our faith instead of our physical existence, we can walk with God, allowing him to work in us, through us, and with us.

So then after the Lord had spoken unto them, he was received up into heaven, and sat on the right hand of God. And they went forth, and preached every where, the Lord working with them, and confirming the word with signs following. Amen.

MARK 16:19–20 (KJV)

NOTES

NOTES

NOTES

NOTES

ACKNOWLEDGMENTS

First and foremost, I give all the glory to God for the opportunity to write about what his one and only Son sacrificed in order to give his children freedom and victory. I am also thankful to my mom, dad, sister Grace, friends, and my Calvary Chapel Oakville family for their endless love, support, and prayers. I would also like to thank the editors at Penguin Random House (including Caroline Lee, Tracy Donley, and Hane C. Lee) for their patience and perseverance in elevating this book with their feedback.

ABOUT THE AUTHOR

 HELEN H. LEE, MSc, specializes in helping women experience a transformative relationship with God through Spirit-led coaching. She is the founder of Grit Grace Grow Co., whose mission is to build a community of women empowered by God to live and love like Jesus. Her passion is to help women experience emotional, relational, and mental freedom so they can flourish in their God-given calling. Her coaching style is compassionate and client-centered and aimed at empowering clients to be led by the Holy Spirit and biblical principles so they can experience spiritual growth. She has also authored *Finding Peace: Prayer Journal for Women (Weekly Devotions, Prompts, and Exercises for Managing Anxiety)*.

Connect with Helen on Facebook or Instagram @grit.grace.grow.coaching.

Hi there,

We hope you enjoyed *Walk with Jesus: Bible Study for Women*. If you have any questions or concerns about your book, or have received a damaged copy, please contact customerservice@penguinrandomhouse.com. We're here and happy to help.

Also, please consider writing a review on your favorite retailer's website to let others know what you thought of the book!

Sincerely,
The Zeitgeist Team